DEATH
AND DISASTER
IN VICTORIAN TELFORD

ALLAN FROST

AMBERLEY PUBLISHING

The 1968 Telford area, showing places mentioned in this book.

First published 1995 (two editions)
This edition 2009

Amberley Publishing Plc
Cirencester Road, Chalford,
Stroud, Gloucestershire, GL6 8PE

www.amberley-books.com

British Library Cataloguing in Publication Data.
A catalogue record for this book is available from the British Library.

ISBN 978 1 84868 389 1

Typesetting and Origination by Amberley Publishing
Printed in Great Britain

CONTENTS

	A Word to the Living	5
Chapter 1	Death and the Victorians	7
Chapter 2	Superstitions	13
Chapter 3	Ballads	17
Chapter 4	The Death Rôle of Newspapers	26
Chapter 5	A Death in the Family	38
Chapter 6	Undertaking	46
Chapter 7	The Day of the Funeral	56
Chapter 8	Burial Grounds	64
Chapter 9	Memento Mori	73
Chapter 10	Death Reaps Grimly	83
Chapter 11	Suicide and Murder!	91
Chapter 12	Mining Deaths	98
Chapter 13	The Dark Lane Pit Disaster	104
Chapter 14	The Lane Pits Disaster, Madeley	111
Chapter 15	The Springwell Pit Disaster, Dawley	117
Chapter 16	The Donnington Wood Pit Disaster	123
Chapter 17	Further Reading	128

With illustrations from contemporary sources,
private collections and by the author.

DEDICATED

To the ghosts of my past and the skeletons in my cupboard.
May they Rest In Peace.

Jonathan Skin —— came to h*is* death, do upon their Oaths present and say that the said *Jonathan Skin on the 11th day of February 1890. was found dead in the Wrekin Reservoir in the parish of Wellington aforesaid having thrown himself therein whilst temporarily insane.*

Extract from a verdict of suicide at an 1890 inquest held at the Red Lion public house, High Street, Wellington. Inquests were frequently held in public houses which often had rooms large enough to accommodate small gatherings.

Victorian hearse with ornate carvings for hire from William Pearce's Ercall Hotel, Market Street, Wellington. It was put on display at Derek Copeland's sheds and gardening supplies premises on Bennett's Bank, Wellington, in the early 1960s.

A WORD TO THE LIVING

Death is the most traumatic event each and everyone of us will experience. Because the population of Britain is greater now than it has ever been, more deaths inevitably occur than hitherto. However, our culture changed so dramatically during the last century that the impact of a death on the local population is probably far less than in the past, except, of course, for a bereaved family.

There are many reasons for this, which are well outside the scope of this book. Death is, by and large, something which holds a deep fascination for us and which at the same time causes a feeling of unease. It has been said many times that death in itself is not so much feared as is the process of dying.

The catalyst which sparked off my own interest in the deaths and disasters of Victorian times was the sight of a gravestone in the churchyard at All Saints', Wellington, Shropshire. It records the death of four of my great-great-grandfather's children as the result of an explosion in March 1839. It's a sobering thought that, had my great-grandfather (who was about to be born in the house at the time) been one of the casualties, I should not be here today and this book would not have been written. My research into the event led me to the superstitions surrounding death, its numerous causes and the events which followed, all of which are detailed in the following pages.

Whereas Telford as a township did not exist in Victorian times, its original 1968 boundary provides a convenient area upon which to concentrate. Much of what is written applied to many parts of England during the period, but the events mentioned here relate solely to this district.

I have quoted freely from newspaper articles of the period. I make no apology for this; I believe readers will be fascinated not only with the content but also by the style of reporting, which gives more insight into the attitudes prevalent in those days; the manner in which events are reported is in itself an important aspect of local history. Reading old newspapers can be an interesting pastime in itself. I crave the reader's indulgence for any minor inaccuracies which may have found their way onto these pages; they are not intentional.

I should like to record my appreciation to both Ian Allison and my wife Dorothy for their painstaking work in copying numerous newspaper articles, resisting all temptation to correct the original spelling, grammar and typographic mistakes when preparing this book for its first edition.

Allan Frost
Priorslee

Harry Edwards & Sons arrange a double funeral, seen here on Mill Bank, Wellington. Funerals such as this, with horse drawn hearses, were a common sight until the Great War, after which motorised transport gradually became the norm.

A romantically sanitised middle class view of working conditions down coal mines. The reality was considerably different. From a *Hobson's Almanack & Directory of Wellington*.

I

DEATH AND THE VICTORIANS

Queen Victoria, Britain's longest reigning monarch, was born in 1819. The daughter of George III's fourth son Edward, she ascended to the British throne on 20 June 1837 after the death of her uncle, William IV, and died on 22 January 1901. She lived a good deal longer than many of her subjects, a fact not altogether surprising when the social conditions suffered by the majority of the population are taken into account.

Victorian Britain was a time of great change: advances in science, agricultural techniques, manufacturing processes and a Parliament which, for the first time in our history, was forced to sit up and take notice of the voices of ordinary people; these and other factors played a part in the development of the Victorian economy and social structure. Victorians loved law and order, provided it protected the interests of the middle and upper classes.

Unfortunately, from the outset, many of those in authority had little regard for the working class, except to provide them with a moderately acceptable standard of living so that they would labour that much harder. Lowly workmen, women or children were seldom more than 'tools that talk', with few aspirations or opportunity to rise above their proper station. Human life was a cheap, disposable asset – but only if it belonged to a class lower than one's own. Such bigotry and selfishness would undergo a remarkable change by the time Victoria was laid to rest.

Many acts of parliament were passed and much discussion on how matters could be 'improved' for the good of the country took place in the local and national press, coffee houses and hostelries. For probably the first time in our history, people were not only able to speak their mind, but did so. However, in spite of many improvements to working hours and conditions and social amenities, there was still a great divide between the haves and have-nots, a situation which became confused by large numbers of (in particular) men and their families drifting from one social level to another, depending on how their fortunes fared.

There was one aspect of life which, on the face of it at least, ought to have been an impartial leveller – death. Yet it is this most common feature of human existence which served to emphasise the deep divisions in Victorian society. If you were rich, you could afford to die; if you were poor, you couldn't.

At the beginning of the Victorian period, men of wealth and aspiration held the controls of power. They were very conscious of their position in society. They owned much of the land; they owned or leased many of the factories; they dreaded failure and poverty and social degradation. Success was everything. And, since the Napoleonic Wars, wealth brought taxation.

It was inevitable that these same men were reluctant to pay a penny more tax than was absolutely necessary. They questioned every aspect of where their taxes were being spent and were most concerned to find that much of it was being used to support the poor and needy. Something would have to be done about it. Fast.

The poorer classes were always sitting ducks when it came to reducing relief supplied by the System. They weren't important enough to influence government opinion, and had to do as they were told. Theirs were the hardest of all lives and, generally speaking, because there were so many of them, they were forced to accept meagre wages and filthy living conditions as a matter of course. It was not until later in the nineteenth century that wiser folk, who could see the adverse effects of these social injustices, were in a position to voice their concerns and thus influence public opinion to improve matters. Hesba Stretton's books are a case in point; born in Wellington in 1832, she became internationally famous for writing about the plight of the poor and other social injustices, so much so that she gained support from folk who had the power to pressure Parliament into changing laws.

Perhaps the most damning indictment of Parliament was its treatment of the poor, that mass of unfortunates who, often through no fault of their own, were forced to seek assistance from the state. The government saw fit to change the rules concerning poor relief by making workhouses the ultimate in last resorts. The object of the workhouse 'test' was to reduce the level of taxation by limiting the number of paupers seeking relief, despite an increasing population. People would need to be desperate to enter their dreaded doors. Workhouses were run under the harshest regimes. Personal freedoms were non-existent. Families and children were split up. The quality and quantity of daily food was barely enough to keep flesh on weak bones. Uniforms had to be worn at all times, just like in prison except that prison was preferable. At least release was possible from a prison. Once accepted in the workhouse, a stroke of good fortune was, so many believed, the only means of escape. Unless you died. Death in the workhouse was to be feared and despised; it was the ultimate in human indignity. Things were about to get worse. Much worse.

Remnants of the former Union Workhouse in Walker Street, Wellington, erected sometime after 1797. In 1875 the workhouse occupied new premises on Holyhead Road and subsequently became Wrekin Hospital and these buildings later became the Union Brewery and currently comprise part of the town library.

A VARIETY OF SUBJECTS ALWAYS READY FOR MEDICAL STUDENTS

DISSECTION

THE POOR MANS CONVOY

Straight from the workhouse to the dissecting table: from Augustus Pugin's *Contrasted Residences for the Poor*, 1841.

Since Henry VIII's reign, the corpses of executed felons could legally be handed over to 'anatomists' and 'physics' for examination, in an effort to learn more about disease and the human body. The felon, having endangered society with his outrageous acts, could have no objection if his body were donated for the good of society as recompense for his atrocities after he had finished with it.

More and more surgeons needed corpses upon which to experiment and the supply of subjects from the prisons was not nearly enough to satisfy demand. 'Body snatching', as in the infamous Burke and Hare affair of the 1820s, was apparently rife in cities and even some towns. Something had to be done if medical research were to flourish without tarnishing its 'good name'.

The implications of the subsequent Anatomy Acts of 1831 and 1832 were terrifying to the working classes who, because of seasonal fluctuations in labour requirements in mines, factories and on the land, had come to expect at least a short spell in the workhouse while they waited for more work to come their way. If they were to die while in receipt of relief, they could expect a pauper burial paid for by the parish. This was something with which they had come to terms over the years.

The Anatomy Acts added a new dimension to the stigma; if any person died in a workhouse, they would still receive, in theory at least, a pauper burial, but their body would thereafter be forfeit to local surgeons who could use it as they saw fit in the interests of anatomical research. Dismemberment. Dissection. Experimentation. Organs preserved in glass jars. In a single stroke, the government had equated poverty with offences punishable by execution. The anatomists were very happy. The working classes were utterly devastated. They envisaged a short journey from the workhouse to the dissecting room.

By the time Victoria came to the throne, the Anatomy Acts were well established. The prospect of death in the workhouse was the most feared end to a human life. Death outside the workhouse, whatever the extent of destitution and personal misery, was much more preferable. Death was the 'Poor Man's Friend' (below, as depicted in a *Punch* magazine), especially if it meant his body could escape the saws, knives and jars of the medical men.

Many parishes, such as those in the present Telford area, preferred, wherever possible, to administer Poor Law relief in the form of 'outdoor' relief. They were well aware that many of the calls on their charity came from skilled men who were temporarily seeking employment in one of the varied industrial concerns nearby. More than a few were not only housed but had also been employed by those same companies, and it was a good indication that more work was forthcoming if the employer did not evict the tenants from his property. It made both economic and social sense to pay a small amount of dole money to a man and his family, enabling them to remain in their own home, than it would to insist that they all moved into the workhouse, where the family would be split up, the man would lose face and probably not regain employment and the costs of keeping them all 'indoors' that much greater. More room was thus left for those who had no choice but to enter the workhouse.

Yet, to a large extent, the government's intentions had the desired effect. There is much evidence to indicate that many working people did their best to save some of their low wages to tide them over when things got tough. Local publicans and burial clubs started to collect a few pennies each week so that money would be available to pay for a simple burial, even if death occurred in the workhouse. The parish would not object to anyone recovering the corpse from their premises when the time came; it saved them the expense.

Unfortunately, these voluntary funds were not protected by law, and it was not unusual for the administrators to disappear with the takings. Eventually, the government agreed to legislate for friendly societies to be operated on a sound financial basis. These societies performed the same function as the earlier burial clubs; people paid whatever they could afford each week and attended meetings held at their particular branch (that at Donnington was especially well represented in the 1870s, when it was common for about 300 'investors' to attend). Even those with the smallest incomes and lowest standards of living did their best to pay, if only to avoid passing through the workhouse door.

Money collected was invested sensibly and dividends declared. Funerals were paid for out of the common fund. Provided payments were kept up, the investment was safe. These societies worked on the principle that the number of payments made annually would always be less than the money collected, assuming that new investors joined and the capital was invested wisely, a similar system used by modern life assurance societies.

While the lower classes seem to have been preoccupied with avoiding the workhouse at all costs, the upper classes had nothing much to fear in that direction. The middle classes, that extensive band of entrepreneurs, did their utmost to consolidate their profits and maintain a satisfactory standard of living. They, too, always had the prospect of an economic disaster at the back of their minds, but as a rule they had little to fear by comparison. Theirs was a different world, where a man could make a name for himself. Make a bit of money and enjoy life. Do good works. Be respected by his own kind. Have a street named after him. Immortality indeed!

All things being equal, the shopkeeper had the same chance of dying as the coal miner, but the means of dying was a totally different matter. Death was ever-present, especially to the humble worker, who risked his life to extract those things which made the homes of the tradesmen that bit more comfortable. Death manifested itself in a wide variety of ways. However, whatever the social background, the prospect of an early death was always to be expected. Disease, in particular, makes no class distinction.

The middling classes are portrayed, whether rightly or wrongly, as expecting a funeral ceremony in keeping with their status. They spent a small fortune on the event itself and on a fitting memorial to themselves afterwards. Alarmed by the increasing number of working class headstones littering the churchyard, they needed to make an even bigger statement to convince themselves of their own earthly importance (and perhaps continued importance in the afterlife).

There is no doubt that many of this class were an asset to their own societies, and ostentation in death has been a trait over the millennia, but the Victorians seem to have taken it to the extreme. While most in the working class had little time for books or for dwelling on imponderables, a good many of those above them developed a definite fixation for death in all its forms. Doctors and pill or potion pedlars did their best to delay it (for entirely different motives). Philanthropists tried to improve social conditions, particularly with regard to sanitation and employment: remove the danger and death is thwarted. Much good was achieved in practical terms, but from the mental point of view both the literary author and the religious fanatic have much to answer for.

Hellfire and damnation were the chords which struck fear in the hearts of many a Non-Conformist. Heaven in fluffy white clouds if you accepted the traditions of some Anglicans; Hell if you didn't. Religion was in something of a confused state during the nineteenth century, more so when it tried to involve itself in politics and social reform, matters which were for secular men (according to their own parishioners).

There was much religious debate, even within the same religious denomination, yet, in spite of divisions and the number of sects, church attendance was very high, especially at Methodist chapels in the area. Most people had simple religious beliefs which had satisfied them for generations; they were, in many ways, naive and often supported by innumerable romantic illustrations, both in religious tracts as well as in paintings, the latter frequently adapted as subjects for Anglican church windows. There was an element of incongruity between inspired religious art and the suffering of one's fellow man. How religious attitudes were reconciled with the hypocrisy and moral turpitude practised by people from all ranks in Victorian society is not a point for discussion here. The wages of sin are death and we are all sinners.

The problem was simply that the aftermath of death was completely unknown. No single religion seemed to have the definitive answer, so individual attitudes depended very much on how convincing a particular church, priest or minister made his arguments sound. It was all very confusing for learned men, so how could uneducated folk decide which was the path to truth and salvation? It didn't help ordinary people much when agnostics and atheists propounded their opinions; it completely clouded the issue and no doubt caused more anxiety and uncertainty. Most of us need some light at the end of the tunnel, and hope for something better when we shuffle off this mortal coil.

The mysteries of death were most confusing to the Victorian mind. While religious conviction managed to satisfy the majority up to a point, there were still a great many influenced by the upsurge in Gothic horror novels, poetry and other literature designed to terrify the unwary reader. (Many well-known writers of the time seemed obsessed with death. Some folk, often young women, even 'collected' epitaphs and wrote them in their own special albums.)

Death found its way into all manner of printed matter. The full impact and effect of these tales to any Victorian mind cannot be overstated. Wider literacy brought with it a desire to read more, whatever the subject. Nineteenth-century readers loved to be scared and shocked, preferably in the comfort of a familiar armchair with a maid standing nearby clutching a bottle of smelling salts. Listening to ghost stories around the fire in a darkened room at Christmas time is another example of a Victorian scary pastime. This form of escapism was extremely popular but, if not accepted as entertainment, could result in excessive morbidity wherein all matters relating to death, graves, premature burial, unearthly and demonic creatures became an unhealthy obsession. It comes as no surprise to discover that some portions of the funeral trade took advantage of what is now termed a 'niche market', whereby specialist products like 'last chance' and airtight coffins could be

The Dismal Trade involved a wide range of businesses, including Johnson's of Walker Street, Wellington. Mr. Johnson was a blacksmith and wheelwright... and coffin maker. Taken in the early 1900s, the photograph also shows the former workhouse being used as a brewery.

provided – at a cost – to those particularly gullible or panic stricken at the thought of being buried alive.

Everyone involved in the 'Dismal Trade' – coffin makers, undertakers, funeral directors, hearse builders and hirers, shroud makers, timber merchants, midwives, monumentalists, engravers, florists, newspapers, magazines, books and especially religion itself – played a valuable part, not only in serving the needs of the bereaved but also in supporting the national economy.

Individually, they had but a small part to play and their earnings might be low. Collectively, they made the treatment of death in Victorian times a ceremonial event full of tradition and superstition, to which everyone was invited. Sooner or later.

2

SUPERSTITIONS

There have been superstitions relating to death ever since man was first able to observe the activities in his surroundings and draw his own conclusions. The fact that his observations were, in reality, largely misplaced and unfounded, has consistently been ignored.

Superstitions and the interpretation of omens are essentially based on irrational beliefs which have, over the centuries, become deep-rooted and generally accepted as irrefutable truths. Even today many people will not walk under ladders but will give sound reasons for not doing so rather than admit to an uneasy feeling of inviting doom as their motivation.

The Victorian working classes were more prone to foster belief in the superstitions than their more enlightened middle class contemporaries, but this is not to say that the middling classes were not susceptible to its influences.

To identify which of those beliefs specifically originated in any particular part of the country is impossible. Movement of the lower classes from one parish to another and from one county to another had been a major factor in the dissemination of superstitions for well over a hundred years by the time Queen Victoria ascended the throne.

Initially attributed to the effects of the agrarian revolution which led to large numbers of farm workers being dispossessed, the subsequent progress of the industrial revolution led to a far greater movement of people seeking employment, firstly in the mining areas and later in town-based factory concentrations. As the people spread, so did their superstitions; the development of the railway system helping the process.

Many middle class Victorians were intensely interested in gathering facts and seeking knowledge, particularly in the fields of history and social behaviour. It is not surprising, therefore, that some sought to record aspects of common life, not just for posterity but also as a mild form of amusement. Several publications on 'folklore' resulted, often based on artificial county boundaries. Charlotte Burne, for example, wrote copiously on her discoveries of Shropshire folklore and published her work in 1883.

The word 'folklore' first appeared during Victorian times and was used in something of a condescending manner by the middling classes when they referred to those fascinating but somewhat misplaced beliefs of the poorer classes. It was coined by a W. J. Thoms in 1846 and was deemed to be the study of archaic beliefs and customs sustained by the common people.

Superstitions were more strongly believed in and observed during early Victorian times than they were towards the end of the nineteenth century, possibly because of better education then becoming more widely available to the working classes. While many superstitions were connected with or foretold impending ill fortune, these are a few of those which related to death. Doubtless there were a few people with warped minds capable of carrying out some of the actions mentioned.

They are in no particular order insofar as potency is concerned.

⚱ Bees swarming on dead wood or on the side of a house foretold a death in the family of the person who owned the wood or the house. A bee entering a house was a sure sign of death. It was also the custom to advise bees of a death in the family and to give them a piece of the funeral cake together with some beer.

⚱ No one wanted to be the first to be buried in a new churchyard because the first corpse interred was believed to be a gift to the devil. In view of the number of new churchyards consecrated in the Telford area during the 1830s to 1850s, this could have been something of a problem if the belief was widely held.

⚱ The ghost of the last person buried in a churchyard watched over it until the next burial took place. Consequently, enquiries after the health of a sick person were often resented.

⚱ Magpies, ravens and moths were regarded as omens of death, as was a rat or mouse gnawing at your clothes.

⚱ Cats were believed to suck the breath from infants, thus causing an early death. However, cats (and, apparently, dogs) could also absorb illnesses from children and so effect a cure. The poor animals were supposed to die as a result, but doubtless the children were grateful.

⚱ Evil consequences would result from the bite of a dog unless the dog was at once put to death.

⚱ If either the bridegroom or bride dropped the ring during their wedding ceremony, he or she would be the first of the couple to die.

⚱ To name a child after someone who had recently died was tempting providence. Similarly, to name a child after one of its parents was thought to speed on that parent's death. Considering the number of children who were (and still are) named after their parents, this belief was obviously not a common one.

⚱ If you fell ill while in church, death was bound to follow. This was deemed to be particularly true of colds and was presumably why congregations often complained about the lack of efficient heating.

- Sounding the Tolling Bell at funerals was considered most effective at driving the devil away. However, a church bell tolling with a heavy sound or ringing louder than usual was supposed to presage a death.

- The hoot of an owl foretold a death.

- A clap of thunder immediately after a burial meant that the soul of the departed has entered Heaven.

- Clocks were believed to stop at the moment of death. Apparently this did happen with some regularity. Furthermore, if the church clock struck while a hymn was being sung at a morning service, a death would occur during the following week. It was also unlucky for the church clock to strike during a wedding.

- It was unlucky to turn a lump of coal over when poking at the fire. Death or poverty would ensue. And you should never burn wood from an elder tree as a death would result.

- It was necessary not to stand at the foot of a dying person's bed; doing so would hinder the departing spirit's passage to the afterlife.

- Making a ring out of three coffin nails extracted from coffins in three different churchyards was supposed to ward off rheumatism.

- Doors, windows and even boxes should be opened to ease the last moments of a dying person's life.

- A dying person would suffer in their final moments if their pillow contained even a single feather from a wild bird. As a result, it was quite common to remove pillows altogether, just in case.

- The wearing of a dead person's clothes was thought to be something of a waste of time because the clothes would not last long. As the body rotted, so would the garments. Either that or they would pass on any diseases suffered by the deceased.

- Miners did their utmost not to work on Good Fridays; to do so was disrespectful to the anniversary of Christ's death and might well result in fearful retribution.

- Until his body had been recovered and decently buried, miners were reluctant to continue working in the pit if one of their colleagues had died inside it.

- If a corpse was still limp or supple when it was placed in its coffin, there would shortly be another death in the house or family.

- Touching a corpse would prevent nightmares and dreams of the dead. Holding a dead person's hand was particularly effective at curing ailments. However, if the corpse had been murdered and the murderer touched it, the corpse was bound to give some sign to indicate the murderer's guilt.

- As soon as a coffin had been taken out of the house for burial, whatever furniture was used to support the coffin (tables, chairs, etc.) must be upturned straight away to preclude another death occurring in the house within the week. It was also thought prudent to rearrange the furniture in the deceased's bedroom so that, if the ghost returned, it would not recognise the place and would quickly depart, so leaving the family at peace.

☠ If someone smelled roses when there weren't any around, someone else was going to die.

☠ If a corpse was not carried out of the house feet first, the ghost of the deceased would return to haunt the property.

☠ It was considered a sign of happiness in the afterlife if it rained on the coffin during the funeral. However, if tears fell on the body, the soul would have no rest.

☠ Meeting a funeral, especially while on the way to a wedding, was most unlucky.

☠ Leaving a freshly-dug grave open on a Sunday (or during a wedding ceremony) invited a death within the parish in the ensuing week (or the early death of the bride or bridegroom).

☠ Hats had to be removed until a funeral procession had passed by, to save the wearer from misfortune. Similarly, it was prudent to walk with the procession for a few paces, even if it meant retracing your steps afterwards.

☠ Always cover your mouth when yawning so your spirit doesn't leave your body, leaving space for the devil to enter.

☠ If a sparrow landed on a piano, someone in the house would die.

☠ Opening an umbrella indoors, or dropping one on the floor, meant that there was going to be a murder. It was bad luck to lock the door of a house after the funeral party had left.

☠ It was a bad omen if someone sick was in the house and a dog howled at night. It could be countered by reaching under the sick person's bed and turning over a shoe.

☠ If several deaths occur in the same family, to prevent deaths spreading even further, tie a black ribbon to everything left alive that enters the house, even pet dogs and cats, and chickens. (But why would anyone want a chicken to enter the house?)

☠ Large drops of rain falling were a sure sign that there has just been a death.

☠ Beware the three knocks of death! If three knocks at the door are heard and no one is there, it meant someone close to you has died.

So much for superstitions.

(Touch wood!)

3
BALLADS

Probably every area in the country has been entertained by ballads at one time or another, many of which were inspired by local tragedies. Whilst ballads on murders were always popular with the masses, those composed where mining activity was predominant were invariably influenced by industrial accidents and disasters. This part of Shropshire was no exception.

Whereas ballads were known to have existed throughout the ages, often performed by travelling troubadours and strolling minstrels, those which have survived relating to this part of Shropshire were mainly created between 1810 and 1910. Most were apparently composed by the Morgan family who lived in the Dawley area.

Ballads were usually performed in public houses where the singer would be guaranteed an attentive audience. It is not recorded which instruments provided musical accompaniment, but a piano, violin, accordion or mouth organ are the most likely candidates; they were all commonly available and widely played. The style of writing seems to imply that well-known hymn tunes were used to enhance the rhyme.

Money raised from the sale of paper copies of the ballads went to the poet himself and sometimes in aid of funds set up following public appeals for the financial support of the innocent victims of the disasters.

Of the ballads which have survived, the following is typical: it concerns the death of miners at a Ketley coalpit on 6 December 1851; sabotage was suspected.

THE SUDDEN DEATH OF THREE POOR COLLIERS
by Jeremiah Morgan. Price 1d.

Come, all ye people far and near,
Unto these mournful lines give ear,
Which are most shocking to relate,
Of three poor colliers and their fate.

They came unto their work quite soon,
Not knowing of their sudden doom,
As now the pit they did descend,
How soon their mortal life did end.

Pritchard, and Hayward, and Rigby,
Two of them men, and one a boy,

The rope it broke and down they fell,
What shrieks and cries, no one can tell.

It strikes our hearts with terrors height,
In the dead hour of the night.
Some evil person cut the rope,
And two were killed at a stroke.

The men killed dead and boy alive,
But for twelve hours he did survive,
or death to him, as we do know,
Had given a sure and fatal blow.

The news soon reached the widows' ears,
And filled them with sad cries and tears.
As to the spot they did repair,
Their cries did ring along the air.

Now to the widows I would say,
'Cast all your mournful griefs away
And on the Lord cast all your care,
Who always hears a widows' prayer'.

And to the parents of the boy
(I do not wish to pass them by),
'I hope you'll cast your griefs away
and to the Lord begin to pray'.

You colliers lift your hearts on high
To God, who rules the earth and sky.
He only can defend your head
While toiling for your daily bread.

Some early to the work do come,
Perhaps before night are carried home

With broken bones or mangled flesh.
But these were seized with sudden death.

To God each morning bend the knee
And ask His Grace, your guide to be.
He only from danger can free,
From sudden death deliver thee.

To any person that can tell
How the sad accident befell,
They may receive one hundred pound
If out the mischief can be found.

And if they don't confess it soon,
They will meet at the day of doom
And then the sentence will be given:
No murderer shall enter heaven.

May all dear friends now ready stand
Ready for death's cold icy hand,
That when the signal shall be given,
'We all may meet with them in heaven'.

Another disaster recorded in a ballad was that at the Springwell Pit near Little Dawley on 6 December 1872. Further details of the event are covered in Chapter 15.

THE SPRINGWELL PIT ACCIDENT, LITTLE DAWLEY, SHROPSHIRE
On the 6th December 1872, at a few minutes past four p.m.,
as Eight unfortunate Colliers were ascending the Pit, the Chain suddenly broke,
precipitating them 50 yards down the pit, and hurrying them into eternity.

Names
William Bailey, 21, Married. John Davies, 19, Single. Edward Jones, 21, Single. John Parker, 22, Single.
Isaiah Skelton, 15, Single. Robert Smith, 18, Single. Allen Wykes, 20, Single. John Yale, 21, Single.
They were all interred in One Vault, at the Parish Church, Dawley,
on Tuesday, December the tenth.

What a world of care and trouble,
Daily, nightly, we bewail;
The loss of father, brother, cousin,
Of some relative, ...sad's their tale,
Pelsall calamity scarcely o'er,
When awful news comes to our ears,
That eight poor colliers have departed
Out of this mournful vale of tears.

'Twas on the sixth day of December,
At Springwell Pit, sad to relate,
In Dawley Field, in brave old Shropshire,
Eight healthy men met their sad fate,
Their work being done, for home preparing,
And to the bottom they had come,
Little thinking their days were numbered,
And that they'd never see their home.

The band had started, eight ascending,
Cheerful as the noonday sun,
When, little thinking, for a moment,
Every man his race had run.
When, lo! a whirl that colliers call it,
Took its awful course, we're told,
And dashed the eight men to the bottom,
Smashed to atoms. But their souls...

Were wafted, quick as lightning,
To their Maker, up on high;
Who gives us colliers daily warning,
That our end is very nigh.
We who toil and bravely labour,
Hard to earn our daily bread;
We cannot tell the day nor hour,
But what we may be brought home dead.

A fearful sight was at the bottom,
Men cut and bruised from head to toe;
With tons of chain and iron upon them,
Which filled the collier's hearts with woe.
But fear and danger at such a moment, –
Never enters a collier's heart;
So they toiled with anxious labour,
In hope that some hurt, may have a spark.

Of life within their mangled bodies,
To cheer them toiling down below;
but strength and hope had nearly vanished,
Only two could breathe, but lo,
Their prayers to God the only giver
Of life and health, were quickly raised;

That he had spared those few below,
To repent of sin and mend their ways.

So that at every moment,
They may stand for ever blest;
And always ready to meet danger,
To be sure of eternal rest.
So may Christ the Loved Redeemer,
Fit each collier for above;
And unite each one as brother,
And turn all hatred into love.

So that all at the last trumpet,
Will be called to our Saviour's side,
Where all dangers and troubles ended,
For ever there with Christ to abide.
Where songs to God through eternity,
Mingle with the blest above;
May each collier feel the blessing,
With all strife turned into love.

May He bless the widowed mother,
And the offspring by her side:
May He crown the sorrowing mothers,
Fathers, sisters, and brothers guide.
And each day give them grace and glory,
To guide their feet in paths of right;
That when their journey here is ended,
He'll take them to eternal light.

These verses were composed by
W. R. Morgan, Artist, 3 King Street, Dawley
where copies may be had.

No ballad concerning the worst mining disaster (in terms of the number of people killed in a single incident) in the area survives (that at Dark Lane when twelve miners plunged to their deaths – see Chapter 13) but the following ballad was composed after the second worst colliery disaster which occurred at the Lilleshall Company's Lodge Pit at Donnington Wood.

Eleven men and a horse died when they were lowered into pit to start work on a Saturday morning. They were killed by poisonous gases before anyone could come to their assistance. The mine thereafter was known locally as the 'Slaughter Pit'. Further details of this tragedy are to be found in Chapter 16.

LINES ON THE SAD ACCIDENT AT THE DONNINGTON WOOD COLLIERY
SHROPSHIRE
on Saturday September 11th, 1875.

Pray listen to these reeling verses,
Which we now relate to you,
At Donnington and miles around it
There is much grief and misery too
For eleven poor hard working colliers
Went to labour under ground
But by fire in the coal mine,
A dreadful death they all have found.

It was at Donnington Wood in Shropshire
These poor colliers under ground
By a fire in the coal mine,
A dreadful death they all have found.
To their work that fatal morning
These poor souls their way did wend
Little dreaming, little thinking,
They'd meet with such a sudden end.

Down the shaft they all descended –
To labour for their daily bread
And very soon it was discovered,
That these poor colliers were all dead.
Some men both willing and brave hearted
To save the sufferers then did try
They risk'd their lives to search the workings
And a fearful sight there met their eye,

Men who went down strong and healthy
Now were found to be quite dead,
All their troubles they were ended
And their spirits they had fled.
Some poor men and women assembled
When the sad tidings they were known
Friends were looking for their comrades
Relations looking for their own
And when they brought up their dead bodies
The sight was grievous to behold

The anguish of their wives and neighbours
No tongue can tell or pen unfold.
The dangers that surround poor colliers
God in heaven only knows
He ne'er is certain of returning
When down beneath the ground he goes.
We hope their souls are now in heaven
From their labour now at rest
We hope they're happy with the angels
And by their loving Saviour blest.

It is not known who composed these lines.

Murders were also a very popular subject for any budding balladist. Fortunately for the inhabitants of the area, murder was not a frequent occurrence, so when one did occur it was almost inevitable that a ballad would soon follow.

This one deals with a particularly heinous crime, that of brutally killing a friend and benefactor. Although the crime was discovered on 1 February 1812, the ballad does not appear to have been committed to paper until October 1900.

THE REDLAKE MURDER OR, WATCH, AS WELL AS PRAY
Griffis, the Cooper, of Old Park, Dawley, treacherously killed and robbed
his Class Leader, Bailey, after prayer.
Original, by S.T. Morgan. October, 1900.

To all who take an interest
In many a tale or lore,
This narrative I here relate
Of ninety years or more.

From out the grey and misty past
Fresh interest to awake,
I re-arrange this record strange,
The murder at Redlake.

20

Griffis, the Cooper, from Old Park,
At dusk to Redlake wended;
Purpose had he to seek a loan
For scheme of need intended.
Kind Bailey listened to his case,
With thoughtful condescension,
Not dreaming treachery was at work,
And murder the intention.

A fireside chat, a glass, a pipe,
Then did the business follow,
And Bailey took his friend upstairs –
His friend so false and hollow.
And then, to lend him from his store,
Produced his money box.
"Hark!" says the cooper, "It is late;
Tis midnight by the clocks."

Then pocketing the borrowed gold,
He said, "'Twill soon be day:
And, Brother Bailey, ere we part,
We will, as usual, pray."
And kneeling, as so oft before,
Both member and class leader
Approached the heavenly throne of grace
Through the great Interceder.

That was the hour and power of sin,
The cooper's cup was filling,
And murder tipped it to the brim,
For he was bent on killing.
Arose from prayers, adown the stairs,
Bailey in front descended.
And now a shadow crossed his mind
Of the villainy intended.

The cooper's adze uplifted high,
Till now so slyly hidden,
With murderous hate on Bailey's pate
With dreadful force was driven.
Then Griffis, in the darksome dawn,
The dead man's house did plunder
Of valuables and money spoil.
He wished to make no blunder

In Bailey's clothes he dressed himself.
The corpse, so cold and cloddy,
He tied within a ready sack,
To hide from everybody.
So to the quarry's gloomy edge
He stumbled with his load;
His guilty conscience urged him on,
And fear supplied the goad.

He stopped to listen, gaze about,
With feelings wild and dread,
Of fears within the horrors round,
And this burden of the dead.
The corpse rolled down the quarry side,
Then all around was peace;
But the conscience of the guilty man
Cried blood, and would not cease.

For neighbour, brother, Christian, friend,
He'd found this grave of stone;
And Heaven decreed the savage deed
Should surely dig his own.

Then Griffis turned and stole away
From the quarry at Redlake.
But midst the villagers asleep
One woman was awake.
Ironing her garments by the door,
She heard and saw some form
Slink through the light from her cot shown,
With a burden in the dawn.

The scene is changed – tis early dawn
And in the rugged dell
A throng of people gathered see
And still the numbers swell.
The murder's out – the dead is found –
The sack has been untied,
And the hidden deed is out to view
It vainly sought to hide.

Soon neighbours ask, "Where's Griffis now?
How is it he's not here?
He should have been among the first
To see his friend so dear."

And someone called to tell him,
That his mate was murdered, when,
He said, in strangest manner,
"I don't care to see dead men."

The scene is changed – 'tis sunny morn
Upon the Shiffnal road,
And the Flying Dutchman's merry horn
Signals the waiting load.
Down the steep bank, near Oakengates,
The great coach comes in view,
With horses spright and harness bright,
Coachman and Guard in blue.

Some passengers, maybe, alight,
Here near the Rose and Crown;
But one amongst the number there
Makes furtive glance around.
And eager, goes to board the coach;
But a hand falls on his shoulder,
And as he turned himself about,
His heart's blood runs much colder.

"O, no offence, no offence,"
The cooper turned said gaily.
"No, no offence," says the constable,
"Only you've murdered Bailey.
You're in a noose that can't come loose,
Your scheming all is undone.
You are my prisoner, come along:
I've stopped your trip to London."

The scene is changed. In Shrewsbury gaol.
The death bell slow is tolled,
While the Prison Chaplain offers prayer
For the soon-departing soul.

The dread procession duly formed
Moves towards the fatal spot
Where Griffis from his final life
Will get his final drop.

A thousand faces upward turn
To see the condemned man.
A sudden hush, a shudder dread
Through that vast concourse ran,
As the condemned his crime confessed,
His guilt to all proclaimed.
Acknowledged pardon found through Christ,
And peace with Heaven obtained.

He gave this hymn out on the drop
As all the people gaze:
"O for a thousand tongues to sing
My great Redeemer's praise
He breaks the power of cancell'd sin,
He sets the prisoner free
His blood can make the foulest clean –"
Then Griffis, where was he?
Stern justice drew the sudden bolt
In the middle of the song;

The penalty has come at last
And the murderer was hung.
The power of gold! O, who can tell
Its range for good or evil,
For which a man will sell his soul,
And barter with the devil.
How great a blessing, greater curse,
As hearts of men may sway;
'Twill brighten life, or hasten death
So watch, as well as pray.

This last ballad has a totally different approach from the others in this chapter. It does not give the outcome of the murder enquiry; instead, it gives the circumstances leading to the discovery of the body in November 1846 and then tends to concentrate on the police and court handling of the main suspect. That there was immense popular support for the suspect, George Harris, support which was emphatically reflected in his treatment at the trial. We can never know whether the public's opinion was tempered by the fact that Zusman was a foreigner and Harris was a well-known local. In some respects it is a much more mature piece of poetry than the earlier ballads and, despite its length, manages to keep the reader's (or listeners) attention and interest throughout.

THE STIRCHLEY TRAGEDY

Poor Russian Pole, Barnatt Zusman by name
Left his own country, and to old England came.
Employment he got under a Mr. Cohen,
An acquaintance, and one of his own countrymen.

Cohen resided in Brum, and a jeweller by trade,
And by his industry a large fortune had made;
Poor Zusman was appointed his traveller to be,
For three or four weeks in the Black Country.

He gave satisfaction to his master while there,
Who afterwards sent him down into Shropshire;
In an unlucky hour poor Zusman came down,
And lodg'd with an old chum in Ironbridge town.

One morn in November he early arose,
And cleaned his watches – not thinking of foes;
He was going to the Finger, and to Dawley Green,
But never more in Ironbridge was poor Zusman seen.

But near to the Finger some one did him see,
And going directly to Stirchley was he;
It was in the evening, and the clock about five,
And that was the last time he was seen alive.

Near a fortnight pass'd by, when a sportsman named Clarke
Was hunting a hare, when he heard his dog bark,
And scratch over something that in a ditch lay,
And he went to the spot without any delay.

But what met his eye something bad did denote,
And that was a portion of a man's overcoat;
And under the rubbish a stiffened corpse lay,
That soon was uncovered to the face of broad day.

The police were informed of the facts instantly
And the body conveyed to a public close by;
Mr. Cohen came down before the inquest began,
And said, "It's my traveller, poor Barnatt Zusman!"

At the coroner's inquest there was nothing found out,
But that he was murdered was proved beyond doubt,
And afterwards plundered – for money he'd none –
And his box of fine jewellery likewise was gone.

Poor Zusman was brutally murdered we see,
But who did the deed is a great mystery;
May he be discovered is what good folks hope
And on Shrewsbury scaffold have six feet of rope.

It was in the June after one eight six eight,
The police fancied the mystery was coming to light;
Mr. Baxter who had been making enquiries some time,
Apprehended George Harris and Hart for the crime.

They were placed before the Magistrates at Wellington soon,
It was on a Saturday the sixth day of June;
About twelve of the day the enquiry began,
They were charged with the murder of Barnatt Zusman.

A few were examined, but the evidence being weak,
They both were remanded until that day week;
They shook hands with their friends, but few words did say
And were sent off to Salop without any delay.

On the thirteenth of June they were brought up again,
And hundreds flock'd to see those unfortunate men;
The Town Hall was crowded in every part
And each eye was fixed on Harris and Hart.

Mr. De Courcy Peel against them did appear,
But in fairness to Hart he did mention there,
"He'd not evidence sufficient to produce against Hart,"
Who, o'erjoyed with his luck, from the Hall did depart.

Proceedings went on against Harris alone,
Who appeared in good spirits, as you must all own,
And he looked so innocent, many did sympathise,
While tears were standing in hundreds of eyes.

The evidence produced was not of much weight,
And his friends were in hopes he'd return home that night,
But what disappointment when they heard the Beaks say,
"We remand you, George Harris, until next Thursday."

On the eighteenth of June he was brought up again,
And appeared the most unconcerned of men;
It being Market-day, the crowd it was great
And all seemed interested in poor George's fate.

A number of persons were examined that day,
But not one to prove ought against him had they;
In fact nothing criminal against him was shown,
But all was suspicion, and suspicion alone.

An eloquent speech was made by Mr. Younge,
In language most clear and argument strong;
And so nobly did he vindicate George's cause,
That at the conclusion there was loud applause.

George pleaded, not Guilty, and the Magistrates then,
Adjourn'd it to Tuesday, when he was brought up again;
His friends had gained courage, and in God did confide,
And the feelings of the Public were all on his side.

Every witness examined proved his innocence,
(And coupled with Mr. Younge able defence,)
The Public for the Prisoner showed much sympathy,
And expected the Prisoner to be released instantly.

The Magistrates retired awhile to consult,
And the people in Court were surprised at the result;
The Beaks' minds were made up, they'd have no denial,
So poor George was committed to the Assizes for trial.

But that God who sav'd Daniel from the lion's strong den,
Can exert his omnipotent power again;
And George has no occasion his enemies to fear,
If he'll trust in Daniel's God, and his conscience is clear.

Price, 1d   Jeremiah Morgan

More information on the death of 'poor Zusman' and how George Harris fared at Shrewsbury Assizes can be found in Chapter 11.

4

THE DEATH RÔLE OF NEWSPAPERS

Next to the proverbial public grapevine, local newspapers were the most important and effective means of letting the people know what was going on in the world as well as in their own area. While public house gossip might be one way of passing on information, newspapers were able to give an informed opinion as well as reporting the facts of any given situation.

The folk who lived in Victorian Telford were able to buy weekly newspapers produced in (mainly) Wellington and Shrewsbury. Most of the articles quoted in this book were derived from them. Considering the laborious technology then available, they are all remarkable in the amount of information, whether of a local, national or international nature, which consistently fills their pages.

The journals which existed at the beginning of Victoria's reign were essentially directed at middle to upper class readers; very few of the labouring classes were able to read or afford non-essentials. However, as the century progressed and improvements in education (coupled with the minimum age whereby children were allowed to be employed) took effect, more and more ordinary folk took an interest in the wider aspects of learning which can only be acquired through the printed word.

Bible classes, library reading rooms and the numerous workmen's institutes provided more accessibility to those seeking to 'better themselves'. As time went by, notwithstanding the traditional efficiency of information via the public house bar, more and more people were both able and willing to regularly buy a local newspaper.

With its wider readership, newspaper proprietors increased their profits. Because they were very much aware that their readers especially wanted information on particular subjects, presented in a style in keeping with current social attitudes, they made sure that each and every page was packed with as many words as possible. Profits would be maintained or improved if their customers were kept happy.

Details of births, marriages and deaths were, of course, very important. Equally important to the newspaper office was that it should obtain income (in addition to the cover price) both in the form of advertising as well as in those areas where the public felt morally or socially obliged to make an announcement which was probably of no interest to anyone other than a small circle of relatives, friends and acquaintances, but would give the person or family placing the announcement some measure of social importance in their locality.

However, as the newspapers printed their rates of charges prominently in the appropriate column, pressure was automatically put on those wishing to place notices to make sure that the wording was not so short as to make them appear miserly:

1895
Births, Marriages, Deaths, &c..

Announcements of Births, Marriages, or "In Memoriam" are charged for at the following rates (if prepaid): – 20 words, Is.; 30, Is. 6d.; and 6d. each additional 10 words: where placed to account full scale price is charged. Plain announcements of deaths are inserted gratuitously, but when an exceptional remark is added, it is charged for. In no case is any announcement inserted unless the bona-fide name and address of the sender accompany it.

Newspaper proprietors were not so callous that they saw fit to charge for simple announcements of deaths; to do so would be severely frowned upon and cause resentment. But to make sure they were not taken advantage of, anything other than a simple announcement of death attracted a suitable charge. As a consequence of this apparent generosity, the deaths column was welcomed by wealthy and poor alike:

October 1847
Deaths

On the 24th inst. aged 70, Mr. John Baddeley, builder and timber merchant, of Wellington; deceased was extensively known, and highly respected.

On the 25th inst. Mrs. Elizabeth Morgan, widow of the late Mr. John Morgan, of Wellington, aged 86.

Another service offered by the newspapers was that of the 'In Memoriam' column, in which people who had been bereaved placed a notice (usually at the anniversary of the death) to let the readership know that the family had not forgotten their deceased relative as well as to remind their friends of the fact. As the facility became more popular and many people read the column as a matter of interest, there was a tendency to include a simple rhyme not altogether dissimilar to the type of verses which adorned many a memorial stone in the churchyard:

October 1899
In Memoriam

KNIGHT – In loving remembrance of our fond mother, Mary Jane Knight, who died at the School House, Ketley Bank, October 11th, 1897. "Not gone from memory, not gone from love, But gone to her Father's home above."

Short, personal advertisements (as opposed to larger ones paid for by businesses) were also read avidly by all and sundry. Because advertising rates were relatively cheap, all manner of goods were printed. Readers were thus able to sell unwanted chattels, especially those which might have become redundant upon the death of a loved one. The disposal of such items helped relieve the suffering that comes from keeping items which perpetuate a memory:

February 1899

GENTLEMAN having recently lost his wife and child, wishes to Dispose of Mail Cart; never need; will sacrifice for £3, cost six guineas; approval; carriage paid. – Captain Harrow, Stourport.

Newspapers also advertised establishments offering valuations for probate as well as for auctioning the personal and business effects of the deceased:

1848
WELLINGTON, SALOP

MR HOULSTON has received instructions from the Executors of the late Mr. John Baddeley, Timber Merchant, Wellington (deceased), to offer for SALE BY AUCTION, in the early part of March next, the whole of the extensive Stock of Timber, and numerous other effects, upon the premises, at Wellington, particulars of which will appear in future papers and catalogues.

ADMASTON
NEAR WELLINGTON, SALOP
SALE OF GENTEEL, USEFUL, & CHASTE HOUSEHOLD FURNITURE.

MR. HOULSTON has been favoured with a commission from Mrs. Newling (widow of the late Rev. Canon Newling, of Lichfield), who is leaving Shropshire, to offer for SALE BY AUCTION, on Tuesday and Wednesday, the 14th and 15th days of March, 1848, the valuable and extensive variety of Spanish mahogany, rose-wood, and other numerous other valuable effects, upon the premises, at Admaston, Salop. Book catalogues may be had a fortnight prior to the Sale, at the Auctioneer's offices, Market Square, Wellington; at the George Inn, Shrewsbury; the Tontine, Ironbridge; the Jerningham Arms Hotel, & Lion Inn, Shifnal; the Crown Inn, Newport; and at many of the principal inns in the neighbourhood. Sales commence each day at 11 o'clock.

Similarly, announcements were printed by executors and solicitors finalising estates:

1841
NOTICE TO DEBTORS AND CREDITORS

ALL persons who may be indebted to the Estate of the late Mr. WILLIAM PICKIN, of Wellington, and of Wrockwardine, in this county, deceased, are particularly requested forthwith to pay the amount of their respective debts to me; and all persons having any claim upon the said Estate, are also requested to transmit to me full particulars of such claim whether the same may have been previously made or not. By order of the Executrix. FREDERICK BUCKLE. Wellington, Salop, 11th Aug. 1841.

It was very important when the proprietor of a business died to let the public know that trade was continuing. It was vital for previously regular customers to maintain their support, otherwise the business could fold.

Realising that, because of the layout of articles and advertisements in the newspaper, not everyone would look at the business and trade announcements, some advertisers cleverly opted for placing innocuous notices in the 'Personal' column. Whenever possible, they included a personal recommendation from someone of note:

1895

Wreaths, Crosses, Brides' and Bridesmaids' Bouquets, beautifully made. – CHAS. BUTLER, Leegomery Road Nursery, Well'ton. (Ad.)

FUNERALS BY LEDGER & LEDGER.– Distance no object. Coffins made on the premises, 10 to 25 per cent. cheaper than other manufacturers. The following words were used by an M.P.. who attended a funeral conducted by Ledger & Ledger: – 'I did not think that a funeral could be conducted with such punctuality, precision, and smoothness by any firm outside London.' – The Bon Marche, 5 and 6, Castle Street, Shrewsbury. – (Advt.)

The 'Personal' column was also used by purveyors of pills and potions whose purported properties were to cure or prevent illnesses:

1895

THE TRANSVAAL

If war breaks out life will be destroyed. Coleman's "Wincarnis" preserves life. It is made with Port Wine, Liebig's Extract of Meat, and Extract of Malt, and is the finest tonic and restorative to the world; 6,000 medical men say so. Coleman & Co., Ld, Norwich and London. Sample bottle sent free on receipt of full postal address. Please name paper. – (Advt.)

Not all articles were of a serious nature; a supply of 'space fillers' was maintained in the newspaper office which could be called on to fill odd gaps in the made-up pages just prior to 'going to press':

1895

An engine-driver saying that the usual life of a locomotive was only thirty years, a passenger remarked that such a rough~looking thing ought to live longer than that. "Well," responded the engine-driver, "perhaps it would if it didn't smoke so much."

Perhaps most interesting of all were the reports of individual misfortune. Human nature being what it is, reports of calamity are always popular. A Victorian journalist knew he must report as much detail as he possibly could. Newspapers frequently resorted to changing the size of typeface part-way down a column to squeeze in every last morsel of information. Personal accidents were very common, many of which were situations which were only a whisker away from being the subject of an inquest:

September 1862
MADELEY

SINGULAR ACCIDENT. – On Wednesday last a number of people from Madeley visited the Wrekin, being conveyed thither in carts. On arriving at the foot of the hill the whole of the party, with the exception of a woman and child, alighted, and these two were being driven up the hill, when the horses became restive and commenced backing down again. The woman, seeing the imminent danger, jumped out with the child; and at this juncture, the horse and cart, which had been gradually nearing the edge of the embankment, toppled over, and both rolled over and over down to the foot of the hill. The horse was not badly injured, but the cart was broken to pieces.

January 1863
PRIORS-LEE

A boy, employed in driving the horse at the pit where the fearful accident recorded three weeks since occurred, was found in the carriage insensible, having been kicked, it is supposed, by the horse, as a wound was inflicted on the head; but the poor fellow himself was unable to give any account of it. A mishap occurred at this pit in connection with the machinery, which was fortunately discovered in time to prevent serious consequences to life or limb; and one in the neighbouring shaft, which also, we are happy to say, was alike unattended by disastrous results. On the 19th instant the catch at this pit again broke, when the cage fell nearly to the bottom of the shaft, but happily no one was in it at the time.

Reports on inquests, murder trials and disasters were particularly detailed, as the last chapters of this book show, even to the sacrifice of fluent and proper English.
Inquest reports were prone to curtailed sentences, giving the reader the impression that the reporter's pencil scorched its way down the notepad in an effort to keep up with the proceedings.

However, when the subject matter was appropriate, the style of writing strayed away from the impartial and towards the dramatic, as the report on the Springwell Pit disaster in Chapter 15 shows.

Disasters apart, the editors knew that folk were interested in the deaths and funerals of notable persons, of both national or local importance.

December 1874
NOBILITY

DEATH OF LORD ALBERT LEVESON GOWER. – Our readers will remember that in a former issue we briefly noticed the death, at the early age of 32, of this highly respected nobleman, the next surviving brother of his Grace the Duke of Sutherland. Lord Albert died at Beaudesert, the residence of his father-in-law, Sir Thomas Abdy, Bart., on the 23rd of December.

On the following Tuesday the remains were brought to Trentham Station by special train, accompanied by Sir Thomas and his sons, and upper servants, where they were met by the Marquis of Stafford, Lord Ronald Leveson Gower, the heads of departments at Trentham, under-bearers, and servants, and thence conveyed for interment to the mausoleum at Trentham.

The funeral was strictly private, and was attended by the Duke of Sutherland, K. G., the Duke and Duchess of Westminster, Lady Albert Gower, Sir Thomas Adby and sons, Lord Ronald Leveson Gower, the Marquis of Stafford, Viscount Tarbat, Lord Archibald Campbell, the Hon. Leopold Ellis, Mr. E. Lascells, the Hon. E. and Mrs. Coke, Col. Stewart and Col. Ewart (of the 2nd Life Guards), Col. Marshall, Mr. Loch, Mr. Duncane, Mr. S. Bateman, and Mr. Wright.

The Rev. H. G. de Bunsen, who was to have been present, was prevented by indisposition. The service was read by the Rev. E. J. Edwards.

The coffin was covered with black cloth, and the furniture was white metal, the plate bearing the following inscription: – "Albert Sutherland Leveson Gower, third son of George Granville second Duke of Sutherland, K.G., and Harriet Howard, Duchess of Sutherland. Born 21st of November, 1843. Died 23rd of December, 1874. Of loved and cherished memory."

Lord Albert leaves one child – a son.

The deaths of local personages often attracted obituaries full of references to the civic involvement of the deceased. For example, the 1881 funeral report of renowned auctioneer John Barber gives much detail about his civic duties as well as his funeral. It is full of information concerning his life, the funeral proceedings and, inevitably, lists all the good folk who turned out to be seen on such an auspicious occasion.

The author's great grandfather John Jones was one of the pall bearers, and John's body was, most unusually but in keeping with his perceived position in the town's business circle, sealed in a lead coffin (made by a plumber) before being placed in a wooden outer coffin (made by a joiner in the town).

The following examples from 1885 clearly make references to organisations belonged to by these people, as well as those represented at the funerals; notice also the length of some of the reports and the phraseology:

DEATH OF MR. SAMUEL CORBETT

It is with extreme regret that we record the death, at the age of 65, of Mr. Samuel Corbett, senior member of the firm of Messrs. Corbett and Sons, ironfounders and engineers, Wellington. The deceased gentleman had been suffering from bronchitis, at intervals, for a long time past, but was only compelled to seek his bed a few days since. He has been attended by Dr. Calwell (Wellington), and Dr. Burd of Shrewsbury, withstanding the efforts of these gentleman, he succumbed to his disease on Saturday morning shortly after eight o'clock.

He was a native of Wellington, and was the oldest tradesman in the town. He has for many years been a member of the local Improvement Commissioners and the Board of Guardians, and was highly esteemed by his colleagues; his leading characteristics being consistency and candour. Being a practical man, too, his advice and service were more valuable.

At the time of his death he was People's Warden for the parish, a position which, on various occasions, he has creditably and honourably filled. He has for upwards of 48 years taken an active and practical interest in Oddfellowship, being one of the oldest members in England's Pride Lodge, Wellington, and having passed through all the district offices. He was universally beloved, both for his amiability of disposition and his numerous and substantial sets of kindness towards the local poor.

He will be interred in the family vault in All Saint's churchyard. [Below, appropriately fashioned from cast iron.]

WELLINGTON
FUNERAL OF THE LATE MR. WILLIAM PHILLIPS

On Friday afternoon, the remains of the late Mr. William Phillips, builder, and proprietor of the Ercall Hotel, Wellington in the Cemetery in the presence of a large number of people. The funeral cortege left the deceased's immediate residence shortly after two o'clock in the following order: – Juvenile Branch of the Oddfellows, members of England's Pride Ercall Hotel Lodge of Oddfellows, members of the Salop. Loyal Wrekin Lodge of the National Union of Free Gardeners, the Rev. G. B. Vaux, the Rev. T. R. J. Fawkes, Mr. J. T. Carrane: the pall bearers, Mr. Winwood, Mr. Goodman, Mr. Sigley, and Mr. Hart, sen.; the underbearers, Mr. R. Cotton, Mr. Gough, Mr Hopkins, Mr. S. Jones, Mr. T. Boycott, Mr. T. Fieldhouse; hearse, containing the body; the mourners, Mrs. Phillips, Mrs. Pierce, Mr. Pierce, Miss Phillips, Mr J. H. Hart, Master W. W. Pierce, Master T. G. Pierce, Master Andrew E. Pierce, Master Albert E. Pierce, and Miss Christina Helena Pierce, Mrs. Stratford, Mr. Stratford, Mrs. Coleman, Mr. Coleman; the following member of the Improvement Commissioners, of which body the deceased was a member: Messrs. R. Hobson, E. Paterson, T. Paterson, HT. Purslow, F. Stone, H. J. Webb, H. Shepard, and J. H. Slaney; friends: W. Wycherley, W. R. Corbett, T. Corbett, G. Corbett, E. Lawrence, H. Bennett, J. Pierce, E. N. Turner, O. E. Titley, J. Madeley, W. Jones, G. Thomas, J. Large, E. J. Capsey, A. Roper, T. Pugh, E. L. Harrison, J. Maddocks, &c. The funeral service was conducted by the Rev. G. B. Vaux, assisted by the Rev. T. R. J. Fawkes. At the close of the service of the Church of England, P.P.M.G. Ransell read the funeral oration ofthe Oddfellows over the grave.Magnificent wreaths were placed on the coffin from Mr. and Mrs. J. H. Slaney, Mr. Osborne Young, Mr. and Mrs. J..T. Carrane, Mr. J. Hart (Wolverhampton), the grandchildren (two wreaths), Mr. J. Wood, Mr. and Mrs. T. Corbett (Shrewsbury), Mr. Edward Goodman and Mrs. John Quaterman (Worcester), Mr. and Mrs. W. Pierce, Master and the Misses Sigley (Worcester), Messrs. W. H. and E. Edwards (Cardiff), Mrs. Strafford, sister of the deceased (Birmingham), Mr. F. Heywood, and J. H. Hart. A beautiful cross of white camellias with a cross of white violets within the larger one, was the tribute of Mrs. and Miss Phillips. Mr. Thomas Pearce, Crown Street, Wellington, sent a very nice cross. Mr. T. Edwards was the coffin maker, the coffin being of panelled oak, with mediaeval furniture. The inscription on the plate was as follows: – "William Phillips; born, July 17th, 1826; died, March 23rd, 1885." The undertakers were Messrs. J. and E. Webb.

June 1885
COALBROOKDALE

FUNERAL OF THE LATE MRS. HENRY DICKINSON The mortal remains of the late Mrs. Henry Dickinson, who died on Tuesday, at her residence in Liverpool, were laid in their last resting place, on Friday, at Friends' Meeting House, Coalbrookdale. The body of the deceased lady was brought from Liverpool to Wellington by train, and from Wellington it was conveyed to the graveyard at the Friends' Meeting House by hearse, where it was met by a large number of relatives and friends, together with the members of the Mothers' Sewing Meeting, of which she was the founder. The coffin, which was covered with wreaths of the choicest flowers, was of polished oak, with brass bearings.

The news of the deceased lady's death was received by the inhabitants of Ironbridge and the vicinity with deep regret, for while she resided at East Field House, by her many philanthropic and benevolent acts, she had greatly endeared herself to all, especially the poor. h will be remembered that it was through the instrumentality of this lady that a "British Workman's House" was started at Madeley Wood, which has since been brought down to the Wharfage, but this was only one of the very many charitable acts of kindness she so willingly and heartily performed while residing in this neighbourhood, and her memory will be dearly cherished by all who knew her.

Funerals of not-so-well-known people from the area were also reported, but much more briefly. At best the article would consist almost entirely of the order of attendees at the funeral or draw attention to some snippet of information worthy of note:

October 1865
IRONBRIDGE

DEATH OF A CENTENARIAN: – On Thursday morning Mr. Richard Rothing, sen., departed this life at the residence of his son Richard, who resides near the Bower-yard. This old man had reached the patriarchal age of one hundred years and three months. During his long life he enjoyed the precious blessing of good health. He was the only living person in this neighbourhood, and perhaps the only survivor of all those, who were in anyway employed in the erection of the ironbridge. This iron-bridge was erected in 1777. Mr. Rothing, when a lad, was engaged in getting out the foundation on the Benthall side of the river.

April 1895
MADELEY

FUNERAL OF AN OLD INHABITANT. – The remains of Mr. William Harper, who died last week at the age of 89, were on Monday buried in the family vault at the Parish Churchyard. The mournful cortege left the house in the following order: – Rev. G. E. Yate (vicar), Rev. J. Jobbling (curate), Mr. J. W. Fletcher, and Mr. Edward Clarke; bearers, Messrs. J. Bailey, R. Shepherd, J. Jones, G. Alien, T. Barkley, R. Mountain, G. Allen, and A. Dudley; hearse, containing body; mourners, Rev. E. Jenkins, Messrs. J. Jenkin, W. W. Mannion, E. Jenkins, W. Taylor, and Cartwright; friends, Alderman A. B. Dyas, Messrs. E. Fletcher, T. Guy, P. Pope, W. Stodd, J.D. Benbow, Poole, Downes, and the tenants.

Newspapers did not just publish stories to improve their circulation figures; they also provided a very necessary and much appreciated service when launching appeals to benefit the unfortunate victims of catastrophes.

In particular, survivors of industrial calamities welcomed any relief which would serve to ease their straitened circumstances. Newspaper appeals were, as a rule, very successful and brought donations from as far as the circulation the newspaper reached, abroad as well as county wide. Major disasters would, of course, raise much more money than the misfortunes of a small, respected family, but society at large recognised that unhappy circumstances could inflict themselves on the best and most hard-working folk.

A request for money to be raised would usually be made by one of the victim's friends or the local vicar, as was this letter which was printed in the *Shrewsbury Chronicle*; it sought to raise funds with which Richard Frost and his surviving family could rebuild their home and lives.

MARCH 1839 KETLEY

FATAL CALAMITY

To the Editor of the Shrewsbury Chronicle. Ketley, March 12th, 1839.

Sir. – Will you please to make known to the public through the medium of your widely circulated paper, a most fatal accident that has taken place at the New Dale, near to Ketley, in the parish of Wellington.

Richard Frost, a religious and industrious Collier with a large family of eight children, his wife also near her confinement, had left his home on Saturday morning March 9th, and descended into one of the coal pits in the neighbourhood to work; after he had left home a workwoman had been sent for some gunpowder used in blasting some part of the coal mines, and which was kept in the cellar, the wife ill in bed, also two boys in bed that had been working the previous night. The workwoman after she had taken what powder she wanted, incautiously left the remainder in the kitchen where there were several small children. The powder from some cause unknown, exploded, and has blown down nearly the whole of the house, three stories high; the mother ill in bed, and the boys that had been working the previous night, were blown off the bed but were very little hurt, most miraculously escaping with their lives; three of the smaller children are dead, and another not likely to survive. The mother is lying at the house of Samuel Simkins, a charitable Member of the Society of Friends, insensible of what has taken place. A subscription is being made for the poor man, who prior to this misfortune had become much embarrassed from causes over which he had no control.

Mr Editor, – May I be permitted to say that should any of the readers of your paper or other benevolent persons feel disposed to relieve the distresses of one of that class of men, and a most deserving character, that labours in the bowels of the earth to procure fuel so essential to the comforts of life, the smallest donation will be most thankfully received, and I am persuaded that I need not ask you the favour of receiving those donations as you have been ready to assist the distressed. Your obedient Servant, THE WRITER ED. Any Donations will be received and acknowledged at the Office of this Newspaper.

And this report, covering the same event, appeared in the *Salopian Journal*:

MARCH 1839

KETLEY

INQUESTS. – The following inquests were taken before Joseph Dicken, Gent. coroner, last week: – On the body of Elizabeth Frost, aged 13 years, Mary Ann Frost, aged 10 years, and John Frost, aged 1 year and 9 months, near Ketley. – The father of the children had gone to work at the pit, leaving the family at home, and sent a young woman to fetch him some gunpowder in a bottle.

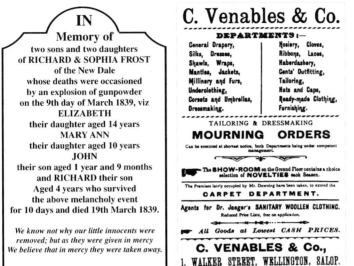

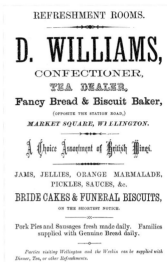

She went to his house, and asked the deceased Elizabeth Frost for the powder, which she brought from a room into the house-place, and put it on an arm chair, and gave the powder to the young woman. She asked her where Mrs Frost was, and she was answered that she and the rest of the family were in bed. The young woman then left the house to take the powder to the father. She had no sooner taken it to the pit than she heard a crash, and going to the bank she saw the house was fallen down, Mrs. Frost and 6 or 7 children being therein at the time, all of whom were injured, but are likely to recover, except those mentioned.

Finally, readers liked to see amusing articles that had appeared in the newspaper many years before. This example from Shrewsbury appeared in 1885:

A CURIOUS LETTER FROM SHREWSBURY IN 1763. The following copy of a letter from Edward Leake, of Shrewsbury, turner and coffin maker, to Jeremy Upton, alias Jerry Bolas, was found some time ago in a solicitor's office…

Sir, – I have been lately informed that you now live at Plymouth and in looking over my books I find that you stand indebted to me in the sum of 12/6. As it is a debt of old standing you may possibly have forgot it, but when I inform you of the particulars I daresay you will remember the charge. It happened that in the year 1741 you were tried and condemned to death at the March Assizes in Shrewsbury for the murder of your wife and in such a dreadful situation you stood in need of a coffin.

In those days as the surgeons had then no legal right to the body as they now have I sold and delivered the said coffin with brass nails to you in the county gaol, but I have not yet been paid for it nor had I the coffin again, for if you remember after your good friends had procured your respite, you, though alive, made use of the coffin by dressing up a fellow in a white sheet and showing him as representing yourself after you were hanged and by taking a penny each person for the show you made a pretty hand of my coffin.

After that play was over, by way of a farce, you converted the coffin into a pair of knockers and used them at play in the gaol yard till such time you were ordered for transportation

for life. As you are now returned and live in Plymouth I have taken the liberty of drawing on you for the said 12/6 payable to Mr Greensill Thompson, which, as I doubt not, you will duly honour, and I hope you will consider me something for interest which will greatly oblige.
Sir, your humble servant and coffin maker,
EDWARD LEAKE
To Mr Jere Upton in Plymouth.

Shropshire (TO WIT) | An Inquisition indented taken for Our Sovereign Lady the Queen at the House of *John Wesley Spragg* known by the sign of *The Red Lion* at *Street Lane Wellington* – in the Parish of *Wellington* in the County of Salop, on the *Sixteenth* – day of *January* in the year of our Lord One Thousand Eight Hundred and ~~Eighty~~ *Ninety One* before ~~JOHN BIDLAKE~~ *John Vernon Thomas Lander*, Esquire, one of the Coroners of our said Lady the Queen for the said County, on view of the body of *William Blockley* ——— now lying dead upon the Oaths of the several Jurors whose names are hereunder written and seals affixed, good and lawful men of the said County, duly chosen and who being now here duly sworn and charged to enquire for our said Lady the Queen when, how, and by what means the said *William Blockley* — came to h*is* death, do upon their Oaths present and say that the said *William Blockley on the 15th day of January 1891. at the Parish of Wellington aforesaid was accidentally killed by being run over with a Waggon*

Unexpected deaths had to be investigated by an inquest and a verdict reached.

Sketch of the chapel in Wellington town cemetery, 1890s. The cemetery came into being in 1875 because the traditional graveyard at All Saints parish church had, after several hundred years of intensive use, become overcrowded and a hazard to public health.

5
A DEATH IN THE FAMILY

The family have just realised that their relative has passed away, fallen off his perch, departed this life; in short, died. (There have always been euphemisms for death, some less objectionable than others.) They have been watching over the dying person for several days and nights, listening to laboured breathing and speaking in hushed tones. The last gasp for breath, when it eventually came, caught them completely by surprise. With a quiet comment like, 'have a safe journey' and a few consolatory hugs, the family prepare themselves for intrusion by outsiders. Now begins a short period of intensive activity riddled with social observances and practices.

The doctor is the first to be called. He is obliged by law to carry out a post mortem examination on the body. It helps that he has been attending to the deceased for some time, so the demise was to be expected. If it hadn't, he might have had to ask a lot of awkward questions, make a few incisions with his knife and even refer the matter to the coroner for a full inquest which would have to be held at the nearest public house the following day. *Actually, this house would be quite suitable in which to perform a brief autopsy; it has plenty of rooms and I could work in one of them undisturbed. Not like that family of seven poor folk who live up the road in a two-roomed hovel with dirt on the floor. Small wonder they catch everything that's going around.*

Anyway, there are no suspicious circumstances that he can see, so he willingly completes a certificate detailing the causes of death, as he sees them, and hands it to the relatives. They can now register the death with the registrar and obtain a formal Death Certificate to allow burial to take place and a claim made on the Friendly or Burial Society.

Someone from the family runs to the coffin-maker's (or undertaker's) and asks him to come round to the house without delay. Someone else goes to the local midwife's and bids her attend to the body, also without delay. If they don't send for her the coffin maker will, and he'll charge extra for the service.

The midwife is first to arrive. Wielding her coffin-shaped laying-out board and an old bag containing a crumbling bar of soap and a small supply of wadding, she asks for a supply of (preferably) hot water and some clean cloths with which to wash the body. Everyone else is ushered out of the room. It's best that the family, in their understandable distressed state, don't witness her manhandling the corpse as she goes about her unenviable task. They want to see their dead relative in a soul-uplifting pose.

The water and clothes are brought into the room and the deceased's daughter insists on helping the midwife. This is the last duty she would like to perform for someone she loved so much. They begin by undressing the body, putting the soiled bedgarments out to be washed, and continue with the unpleasant business of washing down. As this is the body of a man, the midwife gives the face a final shave. Even though the hair will continue to grow for a few days, it would look much worse before the coffin lid is put on if it wasn't shaved now. Finally, the hair is combed neatly.

The midwife then cuts up some of the wadding she has brought. She rolls it up into small bundles which are deliberately and carefully inserted into all the orifices of the clean corpse. She must make sure that the orifices are not sealed too tightly; a disaster could occur which would not do her reputation any good at all.

Bodies decompose quickly at the best of times, but the heat of summer speeds up the process considerably. If the wadding is not put in sufficiently well, fluids will ooze out and they, in conjunction with the natural build-up of gases, will add to the family's discomfort. If the wadding is packed too tightly, the body will swell up and the results could be catastrophic!

The laying-out board is placed under the top sheet of the bed, pending the arrival of the coffin probably sometime tomorrow, and the body is laid on top. The job done, another sheet is laid over the corpse pending the arrival of the undertaker. He arrives shortly afterwards, but not before the midwife has been given payment and a small tot of invigorating gin 'for your trouble'.

The undertaker voices his condolences and takes his order from the man of the house on what, precisely, the services are that are required of him. Oak or elm? Brass handles and depositum – you'll let me have details for engraving straight away? Good. Time is of the essence, you see, unfortunate as it is but you do understand. Silk lining or ... calico, yes, I have that. Hearse and pair? One mourning coach, I see. Two drivers, of course; no, I have to hire them separately from the coachhouse. The usual two mutes and six bearers? Oh, I see, your own friends (slight sniff and one raised eyebrow) ... so no mutes or bearers, just me in attendance. The service at the parish church, you'll let me know when exactly, seeing as you're making your own arrangements. Mustn't be late for the funeral, must we? No, I wasn't making light so soon into your grief, no, please accept my most sincere ... the body's in here, you say? Good, I'll be back in a few moments. No. I shall be quite all right. Yes, I have brought one of our more popular designs in shrouding, I thought you'd approve. Nothing too fancy. Many of our discerning clients choose this particular one. *(That new delivery was promised me last month; it still hasn't arrived and these are the only ones I have left in stock.)*

An obsequious undertaker presents his card in this cartoon from a September 1842 issue of the *Punch* magazine. Charles Dickens, along with many others, held undertakers in very low regard at this time, not least because they frequently appeared on death's doorstep touting for business, rather like birds of prey seeking carrion.

He presents himself to the corpse. The midwife has stayed behind to give him a hand, for which she may receive a few extra pence. Between them they wrap the body in a crisp, clean white shroud. It is one of the common type; a sheet which is laid over and tucked underneath the body along the sides, feet and shoulder. There are two separate sleeves, tacked only at the wrists; the side lengths are unstitched, allowing them to be tucked beneath the arms so that, with the main sheet, they appear to form a single garment. The corpse's arms are folded as if in repose and the hair combed again.

The body is then measured for its coffin, the undertaker making notes with a chewed pencil stub in a dog-eared notebook. He is then ready to leave and promises to deliver the coffin tomorrow morning. (*It won't do to leave it any later than that, considering the temperature today.*) The midwife departs with him.

The family peer through the bedroom door to satisfy themselves that their dearly parted is ready to receive visitors. News of the death has already travelled up the street and neighbours have closed their front curtains and lowered blinds as a mark of respect. They'd better get the rest of the house ready. They pause for a moment, looking at the drawn and pallid face above the top-sheet. It seems uncanny that the features no longer hold the characteristics of the old man they knew for so many years and – cantankerous that he was at times – they loved. The spirit, the feeling, the rare humour, the very essence of life that made him the person he was – it has all gone. Fascinated and not at all afraid, they withdraw to continue the preparations.

Curtains closed, mirrors covered up with cloths (preferably black), all clocks made to stop and the hands rewound to show the approximate time of death. A few sprigs of rosemary are picked from the garden – some of the guests will want to lay one (for remembrance) inside the coffin. The kettle is put on the open fire and some fresh bread and ham bought from a nearby shop; visitors paying their last respects expect refreshment, apart from which those members of the family and close friends who offer to stand vigil over the corpse throughout night and day will need succour. Ham sandwiches and cups of tea are the mainstay of many a wake, as this period prior to the funeral is called.

Everyone seeks out their mourning clothes. The blacker the material, the better the family will be seen as being in deep mourning. Widows include a 'cap', a simple bonnet, as part of their weeds; the intensity of their loss is measured by how many months (possibly years) they wear them. Nothing makes tongues wag more than a short period of visible mourning.

Men are expected to wear a black suit for a week or so, the women for a while longer. Black crepe dresses are not only uncomfortable but expensive; however, social appearances count for much. The time will come when something more functional – and cheaper will be worn, and for a good deal less time. In the meantime, women, in particular, must suffer in silence. It's expected. But why do some folk insist on wearing white dresses and gloves at the funeral of a child?

The man of the house pays a visit to the curate at the nearby church and makes arrangements for the funeral service, which will be held in two day's time. It should have been three days but, as the vicar points out, to keep the body above ground for any longer than is necessary in this warm weather would probably be more than the living could stand. *The deceased was a Methodist, wasn't he? I'll have a word with the minister; I'm sure he'd like to conduct the service with me, we get on very well together. We're not all High Church, you know. Eleven o'clock will be fine.*

The vicar asks if his own gravedigger might be employed; even though he is regarded by many as a drunkard and a surly recluse, he's a good man at heart who finds it difficult to make friends because of the nature of his work. The organist will play two suitable hymns and one of the new bellringers would be willing to toll without pay; he needs the experience and is grateful for every opportunity. No, the service and burial won't cost that much, but these things have to be done, don't they? Where would we be without them? Quite.

After paying a visit to the Registrar of Births, Marriages and Deaths (all deaths had to be registered after 1 July 1837), the man of the house calls at the office of the Friendly Society to which the deceased had belonged. They note the contents of the Death Certificate and begin to make arrangements for cash to be drawn on the company's bank account after the funeral. He then calls on six of the deceased's old friends and asks if they would bear the coffin at the funeral. They are only too pleased to be asked, it's the very least they could do.

That done, he calls in at the newspaper office to ask if they will publish a brief notice telling their readers of the recent demise. They are only too willing and will do so for nothing; however, there might be a small charge if a report of the funeral is also wanted, giving the names and relationship to the deceased of everyone who attends, unless a personage of note is likely to be present? No? Oh, what a shame. Well, come and see us after the sad event and ask someone to make the list of attendees for you to bring to us; we'll take care of the report and let you know how much, sorry, how little it will be. A bill? No, sorry, we'll need cash payment when you visit.

All Saints parish churchyard, Wellington, around 1900. Overcrowded and crammed with wrought iron fences, grave markers and monuments, it was little wonder it had become increasingly difficult to find enough unoccupied space to dig yet another final resting place.

While in the newspaper office he orders some fancy stationery with a very obvious black border around the sheets and envelopes. His wife will need them to write to her distant relatives informing them of their bereavement. Just before leaving, he notices an advertisement for flower arrangements intended for the next issue of the newspaper, which prompts him to call in at the florist's a few yards down the street.

He orders one of the newer styles of rectangular wreaths full of evergreen leaves, to be delivered to the house before 9 o'clock in two days' time. His wife is sure to like it. The florist is quite chatty, yet sympathetic, and makes a mental note to stock up quickly; the old gentleman was well liked, despite his grumpy ways, and there is bound to be a good turn-out at the funeral.

Is there anything else to do? Oh, yes. Nearly forgot. He goes around to the undertaker's premises where, amid oddments of furniture, doors and other household trappings, a joiner has already started work on the coffin. Did we really choose elm? The oak looks much better, more respectful somehow. Too late now. He tells the undertaker when the funeral service will be and returns home.

The house is full of friends moving silently in a steady stream into and out of the room where the corpse is resting peacefully. The midwife and undertaker have done a good job between them. A few sprigs of rosemary have already been placed on the body.

The undertaker and two men carrying the coffin arrive early next morning. They place the empty box on the large table in the front room (they would have brought trestles if a suitable surface had been absent) and collect the body from the bed, taking great care not to disturb its serene and strangely uplifting appearance. It is laid gently into the coffin, whose fresh beeswax smell helps to disguise the more than faint odour already emanating from the shroud. The coffin lid is propped up in a corner of the room.

With that, the undertaker and his men depart to leave the family alone to admire the coffin maker's art, which will also be seen by their friends. They promise to return shortly before the funeral commences, unless they are needed beforehand; it's going to be another hot day. They return the midwife's laying-out board on their way back to the workshop.

By late afternoon the sun is so hot that the effect of the heat on the corpse is alarming the less hardy or world-wise members of the family. There is an awful smell surrounding the coffin, causing no little distress to everyone coming into close proximity. They've already tried to counteract it by placing a bowl of salt on the body; that didn't work, so they tried laying a clod of fresh turf there instead. That didn't work either.

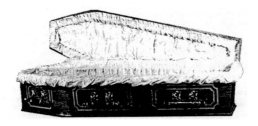

The man of the house eventually agrees to place the lid on top of the coffin and sends for the undertaker to screw it down. After making final farewells rather quicker than they would have wished (the weather is rather warm for this time of year), the undertaker arrives to insert the six screws that will make the bereaved family's life that much more bearable until the funeral tomorrow.

To help pass away the time when there is a lull in visitors coming to pay their last respects, the man of the house collects the deceased's will and other important documents, if they are not held by the family solicitor. As it is before 1858 and there is a will in existence and the deceased possessed more than £5 worth of property, probate will have to be obtained from the Consistory Court at Canterbury; this could take some time, so the sooner the bureaucratic wheels start moving, the better for all concerned. Without the Canterbury Seal the will cannot be regarded as valid nor, more importantly, can the estate, such as it is, be legally distributed to the beneficiaries.

Canterbury Seal of 1847, attached to the Will of Richard Frost to prove that Probate had been obtained and his estate could be distributed.

Family involvement in the death of a relative was often like the events described above, to a greater or lesser degree. Some people, if they could afford it or if they needed to make an outward show of their grief for the benefit of their social peers, hired the undertaker or funeral director to provide only the very best accoutrements for the complete funeral service. Shrouds and winding sheets, as with other services provided for the funerary trade, increased in variety as well as quality throughout the years.

In the 1840s it was still possible to purchase traditional long 'tubes' of material into which the body was slid, with great difficulty, after which the ends were tied together to seal it up. By the 1890s, some coffin clothing imitated the type worn in life, such as ornately embroidered bedshirts with full sleeves; extremely difficult to place on or over a lifeless body, but people were provided with what they paid for. Even death caps and hats. The ultimate aim was to create an impression that the dead were not actually dead, merely sleeping.

Midwives were used by every household in the vicinity at some time or other. These were either professional or self-taught nurses whose function was to bring new life into the world, prepare the dead for transport into the next, and apply rudimentary patching up and general nursing at all other times.

Sometimes they were also in the employ of local doctors and would be first to make themselves available at times of crisis, including the several mining disasters when a number of midwives would be required to work together under terrible conditions. The report on the Lane Pits Disaster, Madeley, in Chapter 14 gives some indication of the frightful circumstances in which they were obliged to work.

Dickens' portrayal of the midwife (Sarah Gamp in Martin Chuzzlewit, come to attend the body of the late Mr. Anthony Chuzzlewit) may be typical of the worst of the breed, but hardly gives a true picture of the high esteem in which many of their calling were held by ordinary folk.

Tales of limbs being broken to force them into the coffin were grossly exaggerated; such events probably never happened. However, the practices of placing old-fashioned pennies on top of eyelids to keep them closed and tying a strip of cloth around the chin and top of the head to keep the mouth closed were quite common.

Bodies do strange things when they die; all perfectly natural, but not something upon which the average living being likes to dwell. Those who provide this largely unseen service to our dead deserve to have the greatest respect and our undying appreciation.

Death was much more difficult to accept in circumstances where the body was not present; both the Crimean and Boer Wars had their casualties, most of whom were buried on or near the field of battle. Emigrants to America, for example, and those at sea were also buried where they fell, often in wild and desolate places or turbulent oceans.

A death in another part of the British Isles might also cause insurmountable problems and added dismay; communication was very poor, even to the end of the century, and bodies were, of necessity, buried quickly. It was not until the passing of the Metropolitan Interments Act in 1850 that corpses could be carried by rail, a means much quicker than slow moving and often erratic road transport. Unfortunately, commercial refrigeration was not successful enough or an economically viable proposition for the funeral trade until much later in the twentieth century, so most bodies were buried in the towns in which they died.

It is much more difficult to come to terms with death if the corpse is absent. We should be grateful that, more often than not, we do have a corpse; it makes grief that much easier to handle.

Receipt for a coffin supplied to a customer in 1869.

Joiner and cabinet maker Frederick Harris also acted as an undertaker. His Church Street, Wellington, premises are seen at the outbreak of the Great War in 1914.

Left: Thomas Corbett was one of many builders offering funeral undertaking in 1900.
Right: Hobsons of Wellington was one of several printing firms producing a wide range of stationery, including memorial and funeral attendance cards and Order of Service sheets.

6

UNDERTAKING

Undertaking at the beginning of Queen Victoria's long reign had something of a dubious reputation, largely the result of greed and sharp practices during the previous decades. The funeral trade was in rather an enviable position simply because everyone was likely to require its services at some stage.

Undertakers did not have the benefits or controls imposed on other traditional trades and, despite several attempts, failed to convince the city livery companies, who regulated the established craft guilds, that coffin making and undertaking should be included in its charters.

The fact was that coffin making itself usually only contributed a minor part to the coffin maker's income. Almost anyone who was adept at joinery could set himself up as a coffin maker; the Telford area was no exception and the majority of coffin makers during Victorian times had a main income derived from joinery, furniture and cabinet making, timber merchanting and even general building and wheelwrighting. Wherever a carpenter plied his skills, there might be found a coffin maker. Quite often these skills were passed down to sons who would later continue the family business.

The funeral trade throughout most of the century was divided into three basic groups: coffin making, undertaking and funeral furnishing. The coffin maker made coffins, but could also extend his range of service to encompass the whole funeral if he felt like it. The undertaker was a coffin maker and always performed funerals. The funeral furnisher did not make his own coffins but bought them ready made (even from as far away as London), dressed them and arranged and performed the funeral itself. Funeral furnishers were apparently quite rare in the area during the 1830s but their importance grew as public expectations from the trade were raised as the century progressed. Each had a part to play as the population of the Telford area increased.

Because there were so many of them in the locality, it was impossible for any to derive a main source of income from coffin making. Competition was too great, and it is doubtful that any would have made more then twenty coffins during the year; hardly enough to support a family.

In fairness to the early breed, their services had probably been developed from helping out friends and neighbours who had recently suffered bereavement. There was so much to do and so much to organise that they were grateful for any help they could get, preferably from someone they knew and trusted. Sometimes the coffin maker would also arrange the funeral with the local vicar, the digging of the grave with the sexton (and filling it in afterwards), the transport of the body from the home to the church and even find pall-bearers and mutes if necessary. But such was the state of affairs during the nineteenth century that the undertaker was unable to invest sufficiently or had no desire to develop this side of his business in order to extend his 'regular' services to encompass the full range of activities associated with attending to the dead on a regular basis.

The less scrupulous of these characters could cause considerable distress to the family who had to pay for his services. Quite often (and the same applies to this day but fortunately there are codes of practice to protect the unwary) the coffin maker was simply told to 'do what is necessary', which is where sharp practices came into play. This (coupled with the fact that the funeral was the last important rite to be performed on any member of society and mourning families did not want to appear miserly) meant that more than a few funerals were performed with a decree of ceremony disproportionate to the incomes of the participants.

Jonas Chuzzlewit, in Dickens' *Martin Chuzzlewit* (published in 1843), was typical of many. Here Mr. Mould, the undertaker, tells the obsequious Mr. Pecksniff about his instructions for attending to the funeral of Anthony Chuzzlewit:

> ... Such affectionate regret, sir, I never saw. There is no limitation, there is positively NO limitation: opening his eyes wide, and standing on tiptoe: 'in point of expense! I have orders, sir, to put on my whole establishment of mutes; and mutes come very dear, Mr. Pecksniff; not to mention their drink. To provide silver-plated handles of the very best description, ornamented with angels' heads from the most expensive dies. To be perfectly profuse in feathers. In short, sir, to turn out something absolutely gorgeous.'... At length the day of the funeral, pious and truthful ceremony that it was, arrived. Mr. Mould, with a glass of generous port between his eye and the light, leaned against the desk in the little glass office with his gold watch in his unoccupied hand... two mutes were at the house-door, looking as mournful as could reasonably be expected of men with such a thriving job in hand; the whole house of Mr. Mould's establishment were on duty within the house or without; feathers waved, horses snorted, silk and velvets fluttered; in a word, as Mr. Mould emphatically said, 'everything that money could do was done.

The undertaker, after measuring its intended occupant, would make the coffin and line it with a suitable material. Until the middle of the nineteenth century it was still quite common to cover the outside of the coffin with a cloth (such as velvet) which was carefully fixed into position with brass or black or white studs. It was not unknown for cheap deal wood to be used, but a charge made for more expensive oak.

The cloth covering could also disguise the use of 'planked' timber rather than the customary single panel for each side. Quite often the inside of the coffin was not sealed, a measure necessary to prevent excess bodily fluids seeping through the woodwork, with most unpleasant results.

Having a free hand also meant that higher quality than necessary fittings and supplementary items could be supplied and charged for – at a profit, of course. Beading around the coffin, elaborate metal handles, a brass nameplate ('depositum'), suitably engraved, charged for by the letter and screwed onto the coffin lid, fine linings and a pillow – in fact, every conceivable article had potential for extra profit, however small.

Other services could be, and were, charged for if the undertaker was given a free rein. There was the supply and fitting of a shroud or winding sheet (which could be supplied in a variety of sizes, materials and patterns); provision of a pall (a rich, heavy cloth with which to cover the coffin); attending to the body of the deceased if no-one else could be found amongst family, friends or neighbours to perform this delicate duty; arrangements for the supply of pall or coffin-bearers and 'mutes' ('official' or professional funeral attendants who usually led the funeral procession) together with their respectful and sombre attire); and the supply of suitable carriages for transporting the coffin and mourners from home to the church, the cost of which was influenced by the number of people required to drive them and the distance travelled. The gravedigger's services might also be arranged.

Even supplies of wreaths and flowers and the provision of a headstone could be arranged, although these were normally left up to the family or friends of the deceased. The undertaker, when required to perform a full range of duties, saw his services as relieving the distress of the mourning family and could expect to charge accordingly. His profits could be increased further if some items, like the pall and mourning garments, could be used at successive funerals and charged for again and again.

The ordinary coffin maker or undertaker could not afford to maintain stocks of every possible item which might be required and so relied on being able to obtain them from other traders in the area. Some specialised articles, such as shrouds and metal coffin fittings, were purchased in bulk from suppliers at Manchester, Birmingham and London, delivery of which was facilitated by the spread of the railway network. The timber was easily obtained from local saw mills.

Some coffin makers provided a reduced service to the local Poor Law workhouses, where a fixed moderate charge would be made for a simple deal wood coffin with minimum linings and a shroud whenever one of the unfortunate inmates expired.

To help reduce costs, some parishes kept re-usable coffins; these had detachable bottoms which could be disengaged once the body was in the grave and the mourners departed (thus allowing the rest of the coffin to be raised and removed), although none have so far been found which were used in the Telford area. Other coffins had a hinged panel at the foot which enabled the body to slide into the grave when it was tipped up.

What was quite normal in early Victorian years was for the Parish Burial Board to provide a coffin solely for use at pauper burials, where the feelings of any mourners present were totally disregarded as the wrapped body was removed from the coffin at the last moment and laid directly into the grave. Some parish vestries tried to lessen the stigma of pauper burials by providing a simple hearse for the use of the poor in the parish; there was one in Ironbridge from 1801 onwards but there is no record of when it ceased to be used.

Mr. Sowerberry, the undertaker in Dickens' *Oliver Twist* (published in 1837) appears to have made a living from catering for parish funerals, i.e. those of workhouse inmates or those in receipt of outdoor relief. His was at the lower end of the undertaking profession and he probably lived in some impoverished back street. The description Dickens gives of Sowerberry's workshop was typical of the time:

> Oliver, being left to himself in the undertaker's shop, set the lamp down on a workmen's bench, and gazed timidly about him with a feeling of awe and dread, which many people a good deal older than he, will be at no loss to understand. An unfinished coffin on black trestles, which stood in the middle of the shop, looked so gloomy and death-like that a cold tremble came over him, every time his eyes wandered in the direction of the dismal object, from which he almost expected to see some frightful form slowly rear its head, to drive him mad with terror. Against the wall were ranged, in regular array, a long row of elm-boards cut into the same shape: looking in the dim light, like high-shouldered ghosts with their hands in their breeches-pockets.
> Coffin-plates, elmchips, bright-headed nails, and shreds of black cloth, lay scattered on the floor; and the wall behind the counter was ornamented with a lively representation of two mutes in very stiff neckcloths, on duty at a large private door, with a hearse drawn by four black steeds, approaching in the distance.
> The shop was close and hot. The atmosphere seemed tainted with the smell of coffins. The recess beneath the counter in which his flock mattress was thrust looked like a grave.

Sowerberry was well aware that his profits could be affected by the death of more portly people – they required more timber for their coffins and the additional costs must be met from his fixed fee. Small wonder he preferred to attend to those with more feeble frames.

Dickens' description of Mr. Mould, the undertaker in *Martin Chuzzlewit*, exposed the almost sycophantic and artificial bearing of some undertakers at the time:

> … Mr. Mould, the undertaker: a little elderly gentleman, bald, and in a suit of black; with a notebook in his hand, a massive gold watch-chain dangling from his fob, and a face at which a queer attempt at melancholy was at odds with a smirk of satisfaction; so that he looked as a man might, who, in the very act of smacking his lips over choice old wine, tried to make believe it was physic.
> … Mould, sensible of having distinguished himself, was going away with a brisk smile, when he fortunately remembered the occasion. Quickly becoming depressed again, he sighed; looked into the crown of his hat, as if for comfort; put it on without finding any; and slowly departed.
> … It was a great point with Mr. Mould, and a part of his professional tact, not to seem to know the doctor; though in reality they were near neighbours, and very often, as in the present instance, worked together. So he advanced to fit on his black kid gloves as if he had never seen him in all his life; while the doctor, on his part, looked as distant and unconscious as if he had heard and read of undertakers, and had passed their shops, but never before been brought into communication with one.

Since death while in the workhouse was dreaded by virtually everyone, it was quite common for relatives or friends of the deceased to club together in order that a 'decent' burial followed by a post-funeral tea would see the departed off without the ignominy of a pauper funeral. In these circumstances, the coffin maker would feel justified in charging a little extra for his trouble.

However, not all undertakers were unscrupulous; many were not out to make a vast profit and genuinely provided a satisfactory service to their clients. As the nineteenth century wore on and reputations became increasingly important if businesses were to succeed, coffin makers made efforts to ensure that the services they provided were what the public wanted and at a price they expected or could afford. They would even arrange for unusual coffins or high quality shrouds to be sent by train from specialist manufacturers in places like London and Manchester.

There was an extraordinary variety of specialist coffins available at the time; lead-lined or made from mahogany, walnut and other rare timbers, even air-tight coffins which helped reduce the rate of the body's decomposition:

SEPTEMBER 1861
AIR TIGHT COFFINS

The "Patent Air-tight Metallic Coffin Company", having purchased and simplified a patent taken out some time ago, are now successfully prosecuting in Birmingham the manufacture of coffins that seem likely to come into general use, when their peculiar properties and advantages are better known. The metallic coffins are made of sheet zinc, with a bead round the edges to impart strength to the structure.

Each one, when made, is tested both as to its strength and the fact of its being airtight, and when the corpse is put in an attendant of the company solders on the lid, although the arrangements for performing that operation are so simple that any ordinary tinker or glazier could do it without difficulty.

The coffin, so fastened, is hermetically sealed against the ingress of air, and medical testimony shows that the quantity of air remaining in the coffin when the lid is fastened on is not sufficient to allow decomposition to progress. These coffins are so constructed as to combine great strength and durability with comparatively little weight; and while they answer all the purposes generally sought to be attained by encasing a body in oaken and leaden shells with an outer coffin of oak, they are much less cumbrous, and are supplied at a far lower cost.

A metallic coffin, of the most solid and secure make, costs no more than a very ordinary one of wood, which cannot be made to exclude the air; although if costly decoration is needed, the patent coffins can be fitted up in a very handsome manner. Apart from the commercial advantages of the invention, it recommends itself very strongly on sanitary grounds, and has been approved by numerous medical practitioners, and other gentlemen in this locality who are competent to judge of its merits. If persons die of infectious diseases, or if from other reasons it is advisable that a corpse should be sealed up from atmospheric action as soon as possible, these coffins can be supplied at a very few hours' notice, even when they have to be manufactured to meet special cases; and if it is required to preserve a view of the features for friends who do not arrive until after death has taken place, a coffin can be used with a glass plate inserted in the lid, revealing the face, from which, as from the rest of the body, the ravages of decomposition are kept away by the exclusion of air.

For those who suffered nightmares after reading *The Premature Burial* by Edgar Allan Poe or similar tales of horror, a variety of 'last chance' coffins were manufactured by enterprising city coffin makers. These were traditional coffins which had been drilled with numerous air-holes and with a small bell fixture fitted on the lid. One end of a short length of cord was fastened to the bell's dapper and passed through the lid into the inside, where it would be tied around one of the body's wrists.

50

If the 'corpse' awoke from a catatonic state before burial it could ring for assistance; after interment it was too late.

It was seldom necessary during the early part of Victoria's reign for undertakers to advertise their business beyond the use of simple business cards; they were hardly in a position to call upon endorsements from satisfied clients. Most of their trade came by personal recommendation and it was not normal to undertake work outside the immediate area.

Advertising was more likely to be supported by the ancillary trades – florists, monumental masons, coachmakers, timber merchants and the like. Coffin makers were an exception, but even they only mentioned that side of the trade as an adjunct to their core business. It pleased the undertaker to see a mention of the service he had provided when a funeral of an important member of society was reported in the local press. Equal pleasure was experienced by members of the ancillary trades when their involvement was also recorded. This, however, normally applied only to the business which had supplied the hearse and other carriages. This example relates to a funeral at Ironbridge:

> The coffin, which was made by Mr. R Nevett, was of polished oak with black bearings, which was covered with a large number of wreaths and choice flowers. The hearses and mourning coaches were supplied by Mr. T. B. Wilson, of the Tontine Hotel.

The Nevett family ran a joinery and building business in Ironbridge before 1840; Robson's *Directory of Salop* for that year mentions The Nevett Brothers, T. John and Samuel, and Pigot & Co's *Directory of Shropshire* for 1841 mentions John, Samuel, Thomas and Enoch, all of Ironbridge, as bricklayers. Presumably coffin making was a sideline which was maintained for many years.

The Millingtons of Beveley, Ketley and/or Oakengates (the name of the location varies in different Directories and newspapers) was another family of joiner-builders who also offered services to the bereaved before the 1840s. Indeed, they went one stage further. As well as supplying coffins, they also acted as agents for a patent perambulator hearse which could be hired, complete with pall and an attendant, for a mere seven shillings. This undoubtedly helped the less well off to raise the dignity of a funerary procession without the additional expense of hiring conventional horse-drawn carriages, thus avoiding the problem of transporting the coffin uncomfortably for any distance on bearers' shoulders.

> ECONOMY IN FUNERALS.
>
> **JOHN MILLINGTON,**
> STEAM SAW MILLS, OAKENGATES,
> BEGS to inform the public that he
> has a
> **NEW HAND-HEARSE
> FOR HIRE,**
> requiring only four or six bearers to con-
> vey a corpse to any distance. Charge for
> use of same, including a pall and man in
> attendance, 7s.
> N.B.—John Millington will shortly have
> several of the Patent Perambulator
> Hearses stationed at convenient places in
> the surrounding district.
> Parish Clerks, Sextons, and Undertakers
> required as agents.—Apply as above.
> Oakengates, February 19th, 1862.

Most funeral transport before the 1840s took the form of either a simple four-wheeled flat-topped trolley with fittings for one or two horses, or a more substantial carriage with a large hold for the coffin and seating at the front for the driver. Various developments took place throughout the remainder of the century, perhaps the most notable being invented by a Mr. Shillibeer who operated from London. He produced several designs for funerary transport, some more popular than others, which were hired out at appropriate prices. A single-horse hearse cost a guinea, a two-horse hearse £1 11s 6d.

One of Shillibeer's most ingenious inventions was a combined hearse and mourning coach, which had a space for the coffin at the front and room for six mourners at the rear. After the coffin had been removed for interment, the front of the carriage and the front wheels were screwed towards the rear of the carriage so that the space for the coffin disappeared and the carriage looked as if it was only intended as a mourning coach.

Glass-sided hearses first appeared during the 1870s, invented by Messrs. Dottridge Brothers of Tottenham and quickly emulated by other carriage builders throughout the country. These hearses were less sombre and proved more popular, allowing the coffin to be viewed as it progressed at a dignified pace towards the church. Thus casual onlookers could judge for themselves the quality of coffin workmanship and see who had provided such an impressive service – metal trade plates giving the name of the undertaker were carefully placed in full view at the centre of the carriage window. These carriages were invariably decked out in beautiful silks and velvet drapery.

One aspect of transport often overlooked was that people tended to walk from place to place within their town or, if they could afford to, bought their own horse drawn carriage, which came in useful for keeping mourning clothes clean when attending funerals.

Carriage ownership and hire became more commonplace as successful businessmen, and less successful ones wanting to give the impression of wealth, took up residence in 'out of town' villas, which might be situated no more than half a mile or so from their place of work. Appearance is everything. However, driving to funerals tended to raise eyebrows as tradition dictated that mourners walked behind the coffin. Unless, of course, family mourners had been persuaded by the undertaker to hire one of his carriages to follow the hearse.

Motorised hearses did not appear before 1900, when funeral furnisher Reuben Thompson of Sheffield built the first which incorporated the 12 horsepower Wolseley automobile chassis. It is doubtful that any motorised hearses were used in the Telford area much before the outbreak of the Great War.

Towards the end of the nineteenth century there was a fundamental change in the reputation and standing of the undertaker in his locality. He took pains to ensure that the individual cost of each aspect of his business was known to prospective clients; there were fewer 'hidden extras' and consequently less acrimony when the bill arrived. Nevertheless, the funeral business was not cheap, but the costs became easier to meet with the general acceptance and affordability of life insurances, hitherto denied to all but a few.

The general standard and expectancy of service also improved; undertakers who were not prepared to accept the scrutiny of their clients were increasingly shunned and the beginnings of respectable funeral directorships were apparent. Steps were taken by the more responsible businesses to provide a full and comprehensive service to the bereaved which encompassed everything which might be required. Competition from the less professional or limited-range businesses gradually diminished as the services of funeral directorships became more appreciated and accepted.

The new breed of funeral directors would prepare the body for burial; make or buy in the coffin; collect the body from hospital, if necessary; supply a shroud; hire the funeral vehicles from a carriage maker or suitable stables; arrange the funeral service, which might include the choir and a bell-ringer, with the vicar or minister, and the grave plot with the appropriate churchyard or cemetery; order the printing of any required stationery, e.g. Order of Service sheets from a printer, and wreaths from a local florist.

There was almost nothing which could not be provided. All the bereaved family had to do was agree with the funeral director what needed to be done (after the costs had been explained) and pay the bill when it arrived. This last point was to be the bane of many an undertaker; it was not always possible for each and every bill to be paid in full when it was issued and several directorships had no option but to allow extended credit.

Two of the longest surviving undertaking businesses in the Telford area owe their success to their ability to adapt from part-time coffin making (with additional services provided when required) to fully comprehensive funeral directing, where sound liaison between the business itself and all the related ancillary trades or professions ensured the smooth running of every funeral they undertook. At last the bereaved could feel happy that the last rites had been performed with decorum and professionalism.

Tom Edwards was a builder and contractor whose business operated from 95 King Street, Wellington, some time before 1885. Coffin making was originally a natural sideline, with oak boards being supplied by R. Groom & Sons, also of Wellington, a major importer of timber at the time whose Shropshire Works premises stood by the railway sidings at the western edge of the town.

Hearses and funeral carriages were hired from stables belonging to the Ercall Commercial Hotel in Market Street. These particular 'Shillibeers' were glass-cased in front (where the coffin was placed) with seating for up to eight mourners behind. They were usually pulled by a pair of horses bedecked with black fittings and plumes of black ostrich feathers above their heads. The sombrely dressed, top-or bowler-hatted funeral attendants, including the mutes complete with black crepe armbands, were normally employees in the business.

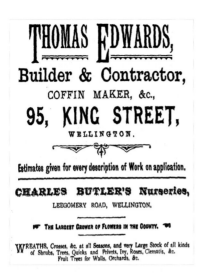

As time went by and Tom's reputation became more widely respected, the joinery side of the business was maintained while the undertaking side expanded. Poverty was so widespread at the time that Tom often accepted payment for his services on the 'never never', where small sums would be paid weekly until the debt was settled. Such was his compassion, understanding and generosity that 'never' frequently turned out to be the actual method of (non) payment.

After his early death, the business was continued, at first jointly by his two sons, William and Harry, but after a while William left the business to take charge of the town's fire brigade then based in Foundry Road. Harry was left to run the family firm with his own three sons – Tom, Frank and Harry – who remained together after his death until the business was acquired by W. R. R. Pugh & Son of Shrewsbury in November 1972. The business continues to trade under the respected name of Harry Edwards & Sons and has since been absorbed into C. J. Williams Funeral Service of Telford.

Another business which originated at about the same time was that of Simeon Higginson Breeze. Simeon was a blacksmith, wheelwright and carriage builder by trade who took to coffin making and later funeral directorship as a sideline. His business was based at Aqueduct but moved to Dawley Bank after his death in 1927, when his son John Vaughan Breeze took it over. John died in 1961, whereupon it was continued by John's grandson who altered the business name to that of his own – C. J. Williams Funeral Service of Telford. (Christopher Williams, incidentally, was only seventeen years old at the time and the youngest funeral director in Britain. He had served his apprenticeship as a joiner.)

Even though Simeon built his own coaches, he hired the horse-drawn Shillibeer carriages from John Sheward of Little Dawley. Coffins were usually made of oak, elm (the former was more expensive) and horse chestnut ('Spanish oak') using timber supplied by R. Groom & Sons of Wellington or one of many other local sawmills. The wood was delivered in the form of large boards (measuring some two and a half feet by seven feet and three quarters of an inch thick) which were stored flat on the ground and separated by long sticks to allow free passage of air between each layer of timber. The boards had to be turned periodically to ensure warping did not occur.

Simeon Breeze.

After seasoning, the boards were cut to size and shape and joined together to make the coffin. Designs of coffin could be varied in accordance with customers' wishes, but the 'normal' and 'fishtail' (where the sides from the shoulder to the foot curved gracefully) shapes were most popular. After assembly, the coffin was sealed with liquid pitch, the coffin being tipped from side to side until all the joints and sides were completely impervious.

The outside of the coffin was then treated with beeswax melted with a drop of turpentine or French polish, extreme care being taken with the latter as white spots could show if there was any dampness in the air or the timber not fully dried out. Additional trimmings and handles were fitted, as were the inside wadding, calico or silk linings and pillow. Taking care that the lid made a good fit, the coffin was now ready for its occupant.

In those days the body of the deceased was invariably kept at home pending the funeral, so the coffin was taken there and the body placed inside with due care and attention paid to detail. The lid was laid to one side to afford friends and relatives the opportunity to view the body when they came to pay their last respects. Thereafter, unless the family were perturbed by unpleasant odours emanating from within the coffin, the lid remained off until it was screwed into place, with six screws, immediately prior to the funeral.

If the family so wished, Simeon Breeze also made arrangements at the appropriate church for the funeral service, the digging of the grave, the hire of carriages and other incidentals. Otherwise his next involvement was to oversee the funeral itself which generally required him to collect the body (in its sealed coffin) from the home, transport it to and into the church, and finally to the grave side. He would also provide coffin-bearers unless the family wanted to make their own arrangements.

There was no legal requirement for the populace to make use of an undertaker's services, nor even those of a coffin maker, yet not making use of them was virtually unheard of. Far better to let those who knew what to do take charge of events. The family had enough to contend with and could not be expected to take on the added work of preparing the body for burial.

That the two concerns mentioned here, Edwards' and Breeze's, survived for so long is a testimony to the need for a different approach to the whole business of providing a funeral service, one which attended to the needs of both the deceased and the bereaved in a way that was befitting and respectful at such a traumatic time.

7
THE DAY OF THE FUNERAL

All the preparations for the funeral have taken place. The undertaker's men have just arrived and, after a final look, a kiss and perhaps a gentle touch from a relative, the coffin lid has been placed into position and screwed down. The family mourners are present, dressed in their best clothes; the men with black silk bands around their arms, the women with black veils and bonnets covering their features. The children wear their Sunday best; the boys with white armbands, the girls with white sashes and gloves, to signify their innocence.

The undertaker's men lift the polished coffin reverently by its metal handles carrying it, feet first, through the front doorway and gently slide it into the glass-sided black hearse, itself decked out with black ostrich plumes and black velvet hangings. They then place the family wreath on the coffin lid and wait patiently for the mourners to emerge.

The men speak in hushed tones to the well trained black horses (also with black plumes on top of their heads as well as black velvet blankets over their backs); the men employed as mutes stand silently in front of the animals with suitably morose expressions on their careworn and gloomy faces. The carriage drivers sit, whips in hand, atop both the hearse and the mourning coach behind. They check yet again that the hand-brakes are firmly engaged.

All the undertaker's men are dressed in impressive black suits and overcoats, black leather gloves and black top hats, each with a black silk band above the brim. Sometimes the mutes carry staffs with black velvet or silk cloth hanging from them, in the semblance of a loosely furled large pennant. It is, indeed, a black occasion.

The undertaker himself glances both discreetly and nervously at his gold chained pocket watch before slipping it back into his waistcoat. At last the mourning party emerge to take their places in the cortege. Glancing back, they note with sombre approval the tightly drawn curtains at the window. They close the door firmly behind them.

They are helped into the mourning coach by the undertaker's men. One of the ladies dabs a cotton lace handkerchief to her eyes. The children sit motionless with nervous expressions, aware that this is an occasion of some note where their customary mischief would not be appreciated. The men sit bolt upright with impeccable dignity.

The undertaker checks that everything is in order and walks to the head of the cortege. So far so good. With an air of solemnity, he slowly leads the small procession along the street, followed in turn by the mutes, his bearers, the funeral hearse and, drawing up the rear, the mourning coach. He notes with approval that the other houses in the road have their curtains drawn and blinds lowered; the pedestrians standing motionless, the men with their hats removed and heads bowed in respect. He glances back to the hearse to note his advertising plaque discreet but unmistakable in the window for all to see.

The cortège turns the corner just as it begins to drizzle. The undertaker turns to look in the general direction of his men and gives them an almost imperceptible nod, whereupon they spring into action. The velvet blankets are removed from the horses, folded and stashed under the driver's seat. All the men clamber silently aboard the outside of the hearse and mourning coach, whereupon the drivers flick their whips and urge the horses into a trot. There is no point in spoiling the velvets in the rain, and the church is some distance away. The neighbours have witnessed the dignity of a slow moving cortege and there is no one of importance to the bereaved family to take umbrage at the increased speed.

After a few minutes, the horses slow down to a walking pace again. The undertaker and his men leap down from their seats, replace the blankets and resume their positions, calmly turning another corner into full view of the church. There is already a large number of attendees awaiting their arrival.

A doleful church bell is rung slowly by the sexton. Its sombre tone is exactly right for the occasion. The vicar waits inside the church, checking that he has his address with him and his Book of Common Prayer open at the page headed The Order for the Burial of the Dead. The organist is playing suitably mournful music from the seclusion of his loft.

The cortège arrives at the church gate. The bearers open the door at the rear of the hearse and carefully slide the coffin out and cover it with a black velvet pall with gold tassels. A single family wreath is gently placed on top so that it does not damage the expensive cloth. Each bearer holds one of the handles firmly and lifts it onto the lych stone, a large flat slab set a couple of feet off the ground in the wall by the gate.

If this were a covered lych gate then the roof would provide some shelter from the steady rain until the vicar comes from the church to lead the coffin inside. The lych stone gives the bearers a breathing space while the family mourners alight from their coach and take up their place in the procession. (The word 'lych' derives from an old English word – lic – meaning 'corpse'.)

After a few minutes (to make sure everyone is ready to begin and the other attendees aware that they must follow the mourning party into the church), the vicar emerges from the church door and walks slowly towards the funeral party. He greets them with a half smile, a simple gesture designed to put these sad folk at their ease.

The bearers hoist the coffin onto their shoulders and follow the clergyman, undertaker and mutes (in that order) along the path as the vicar reads some pertinent passage from the Scriptures. The rest of the party follow, heads bowed.

One of the children spies the gravedigger hiding a few feet away in the bushes. He's leaning on his shovel, wiping his brow with what might once have been a clean cloth. A green bottle of Hollands gin pokes precariously out of his threadbare jacket pocket. It was not good form for him to be seen by the mourners; but it was not his fault that the grave had just been dug. The curate hadn't let him know where the plot was to be until earlier that day and he'd been hard at it ever since. And he'd had to hide the crumbling clay-caked bones of the previous occupant just a few minutes ago. People just don't appreciate his efforts.

The procession enters the church door. The bell stops tolling at the precise moment at which the organ music changes imperceptibly from the dirge-like tune the pipes had been puffing forth beforehand to that age-old favourite, the *Dead March* from Handel's oratorio *Saul*. No funeral would seem right without it. (Chopin's *Funeral March* from his second *Sonata in B Flat Minor* had not yet gained public approval in England, apart from which it was far too short for the bearers to carry the coffin down the aisle before it reached its final chord.)

As the familiar strains echo around the whitewashed walls, the coffin is placed on the black-draped trestles before the altar. The bearers and the other undertaker's men withdraw discreetly outside while the undertaker himself stands, hands clasped behind his back, at the rear of the congregation.

The vicar begins the service. A few prayers, perhaps referring to the deceased by name, a hymn followed by the 'address'. This is the part of the ceremony the vicar has been waiting for. Depending on his mood, how well he knew the deceased or the mourners, the manner of the death or simply how much time he has, his address will be delivered accordingly.

Many addresses are short; some medium length; a few positively long. (There are several examples throughout this book.) More often than not, the clergyman tries to drive home the message that we are all close to death, at all times. Who knows when our time is come? We must all be prepared to die at a moment's notice; are our lives blameless enough to find a place in Heaven? In the midst of life we are in death, etc., etc.

Another hymn, perhaps two, separated by more prayers. Eventually the vicar has finished all he has to say within the church walls. By this time the congregation, let alone the mourners, are so depressed that they are all sure that they are attending their own funeral, a feeling intensified by the distinct coldness in the air and pews so hard that it takes minutes for the nether regions to recover. Several people dab welled eyes with white handkerchiefs.

A look from the vicar beckons the undertaker and the bearers to come forward. They do so and lift the coffin shoulder high after the undertaker has removed the wreath. The church is silent as the vicar leads the people outside, followed by the undertaker, the bearers, the family mourners and the rest of the congregation.

They approach the grave (dug on the eastern side of the church, of course), the freshly dug mounds of soil surrounding it causing a little undignified behaviour as feet try to find a comfortable position. The vicar stands at the head of the grave, the family mourners behind the bearers who are busily threading webbed straps through the handles and underneath the coffin.

Everyone else jostles (politely) for a good position in order to gain a clear view of the proceedings. There is no sign of the gravedigger. The clergyman pauses while the bearers carefully hoist the coffin over the hole under the watchful eye of the undertaker. The vertical-sided hole was empty an hour ago but the rain has since collected to form a small puddle in the bottom. The men and boys bare their heads as the vicar grasps a handful of soil and begins to read an extract from The Order for the Burial of the Dead, casting the soil on top of the descending coffin as he does so.

Then, while the earth shall be cast upon the Body by some standing by, the Priest shall say,

FORASMUCH as it hath pleased Almighty God of his great mercy to take unto himself the soul of our dear brother here departed, we therefore commit his body to the ground; earth to earth, ashes to ashes, dust to dust; in sure and certain hope of the Resurrection to eternal life, through our Lord Jesus Christ; who shall change our vile body, that it may be like unto his glorious body, according to the mighty working, whereby he is able to subdue all things unto himself.

Then shall be said or sung,

I HEARD a voice from heaven, saying unto me, Write, from henceforth blessed are the dead which die in the Lord: even so saith the Spirit; for they rest from their labours.

Priest.

ALMIGHTY God, with whom do live the spirits of them that depart hence in the Lord, and with whom the souls of the faithful, after they are delivered from the burden of the flesh, are in joy and felicity; We give thee hearty thanks, for that it hath pleased thee to deliver this our brother out of the miseries of this sinful world; beseeching thee, of thy great goodness, shortly to accomplish the number of thine elect, and to hasten thy kingdom; that we, with all those that are departed in the true faith of thy holy Name, may have our perfect consummation and bliss, both in body and soul, in thy eternal and everlasting glory; through Jesus Christ our Lord. Amen.

All those who are within earshot also say, 'Amen'. So be it. They hardly notice the bearers have lowered the coffin into the grave while the vicar was speaking, or that the straps have already been rewound and the bearers moved discreetly away to give the mourners access to the edge. The soil landing on top of the coffin sends a shudder down everyone's spine.

The vicar steps out of the way and walks quietly towards the lych gate. One by one, the mourners and other sympathisers pick up a small handful of the soil and throw it into the grave and follow the vicar, who shakes everyone's hand, children included, and gives them the same half smile as he did earlier.

A funeral cortège at Madeley approaches the Foresters Arms public house on its way to the church. The top-hatted undertaker leads the way, mourners carry wreaths and pall bearers guide a perambulator hearse along the road.

The undertaker's men help the mourners back into the mourning coach and take them back home, the horses trot along the muddy road at a brisk pace.

The mourners alight; the man of the house shakes hands with the undertaker, who quickly retires to his premises. He prepares the invoice (it won't be delivered to the family for a week or two, for appearance's sake) while his men dry out the velvets and return the funeral carriages to the hirers. After all this has been done, the undertaker pays the men who promptly spend their hard earned wages in the nearest hostelry. The undertaker is happy; his men performed well, everything went off without a hitch and his reputation is intact. Only the gravedigger is unhappy; he has to fill the grave in as soon as he can and place the wreath on top before he'll receive his wages from the curate. He takes another swig of gin from his near-empty bottle and boots the spade into the wet earth, compacted by trampling feet during the committal. He smiles as he finds an old coffin handle sticking out from the pile; it's a good job no one noticed it else he'd have been in trouble with his employer.

Meanwhile, back at the deceased's former home, the bereaved have flung open the curtains, removed the coverings from the mirrors, restarted the clocks and removed all traces of mourning.

The table is laid with a wonderful spread of food including ham, without which no funeral tea would be complete. Many friends and relatives have made their own way from the churchyard and are chatting happily. Barely a mention is made of the deceased who now lies in his final resting place. The light atmosphere is a relief to everyone as they munch into sandwiches and sip cups of tea or have a small glass of something stronger. The party goes on well into the night until the guests depart to their separate homes. Thank goodness funerals are only permitted in the daytime, otherwise Heaven knows what time we'd all be getting to bed!

A few days later, having read the rather impressive report of the funeral in the local newspaper, the man of the house pays a visit to the local stonemason and decides on a headstone and the wording of the inscription. Blanching at the estimated cost (and he hasn't even received the undertaker's bill yet; Heaven knows how much that will be.), he elicits a promise that the stone will be completely finished and erected on the grave within a week or two. He must remember to check when the time comes; the monumentalist certainly won't be paid until the job is done to his satisfaction. Perhaps it would look nice if one of those porcelain flower ornaments with a glass dome were put in front of the headstone. At least it might cheer it up a little.

All that remains to be done now is to sort out the deceased's estate. Hopefully there will be some money left after all the bills have been paid, if the solicitor handling the affairs doesn't overcharge. With a bit of luck the dead man will be worth more now than he was when alive.

The above was typical of many middle class funerals at the beginning of Victoria's reign.

The essential details varied very little until later in the century when greater emphasis was given to the wreaths and bouquets of flowers (especially chrysanthemums) presented not only by the family but also by relatives and friends.

In the earlier part of the reign, flowers were considered something of a frivolity in such grave circumstances. By the end of the century many of the trappings provided by the undertaker had changed little, although, in this area at least, the mutes had discarded their staffs and swapped top hats in favour of bowler hats, and velvet horse blankets had all but disappeared.

Folk from the wealthier classes would, of course, expect every conceivable refinement to be put at their disposal, for example, more coaches to transport everyone of note who had received formal invitations to attend, a choir to sing a suitable anthem during the service, and perhaps a band or representatives from the numerous organisations to which the deceased belonged.

The Press would be expected to attend in order to make a full report of the impressive proceedings in the next issue. The funeral tea would be extravagant and a striking memorial erected in the burial ground to the everlasting memory of the deceased.

Working class funerals were, financially at least, in a different league. Not for them the extravagance of the numerous trimmings the undertaker could provide. They would either transport the coffin on the willing shoulders of friends or relatives (if the church was not too far away) or hire, for slightly longer distances, one of the patent perambulator hearses (little more than four-wheeled carts with a pulling handle at the front and perhaps two or four pushing handles at the sides).

If certain rigid rules and regulations were met, Poor Law Guardians might permit poor folk to use the 'parish hearse', which seem to have been similar in appearance to the Perambulator Hearses. On the other hand, they might not, as this extract from *Wellington Shreds (and Patches)* by this author, which relates to reports from an 1889 issue of the *Wellington Standard*. It concerns the death of a child; it's impossible to appreciate what the feelings of the father must have been at a time of such great sorrow.

… the child, he [the father] believed, was taken bad on Saturday, and they went to the relieving officer to get an order for the doctors, but when the order was obtained a delay occurred. The doctor ordered treatment, but the people had no money to purchase the articles required. They asked for relief to purchase them and it was refused, but the owner of the lodging-house eventually advanced 6d, which was spent on poultices and other remedies ordered.

After the death of the child, Mr. Taylor, the Nuisance Inspector, came to the place and wanted the father to pay some men to take the child to the cemetery. The woman asked Mr. Taylor to pay the men, but he refused to do so, and afterwards came up and brought two drunks and women with him, and said she must pay them for taking the child to the grave.

Mrs. Moore [the lodging house keeper] said that she would not pay them as she had done all she could for the family by relieving them. Mr. Taylor then said, 'If you do not send the child out of your house by the time appointed, I will stick a paper in your window and charge you a shilling for every half hour you detain the corpse on the premises.'

Then the father said if he could have a decent wheelbarrow he would bury it himself. Mrs. Moore then came to him [Mr. Williams of The Stores] and asked if he would please to lend a wheelbarrow, and he said decidedly he would, and asked to see the father whom he recognised as a decent and respectable man, and he and Mr. Collins gave him some refreshment before he went to wheel the child.

Mr. Collins said the father then put a cloth under and over the coffin, and tied it so that it would not shift about, and the father bowled his own child to the cemetery, and then returned the wheelbarrow to him.

Coffins for the poor, usually made of elm, would still sometimes be draped with a black or purple pall and friends or members of the family would hold edges of the cloth (as 'pall bearers') while the procession walked along slowly and deliberately, led by the undertaker. Wreaths and flowers would be carried by hand. More often than not the funeral would be quite a small affair, but there are several instances where a much larger crowd congregated; personal tragedies, mining disasters and the death of young or respected church-goers would prompt very many others to attend. Small boys were sometimes employed as mutes at the funerals of children, thus adding more drama to the occasion.

What the poor could not achieve with money they more than made up with a show of sympathetic solidarity in the face of adversity. As did the wealthier members of local society, the poor also belonged to a wide variety of religious, social and sporting organisations; all would be represented. Flowers were another tangible and highly visual way in which the poorer classes could show their support and share the grief:

May 1895
THE FUNERAL

On Sunday afternoon, the funeral of the unfortunate young man, James Stanworth, who met with his death at Priorslee Furnaces on the 25th April, took place amid many tokens of respect.

It is estimated that some 6,000 persons congregated in Snedshill and en route to the church. At the house the Rev. J. Pearce, U.M.F.C., gave out the hymn, "We shall sleep, but not forever," which was heartily sung, after which the mournful cortege wended its way to St. Peter's Church, Priorslee, in the following order: –

St. George's Prize Brass Band (under the leadership of Mr. James Bedford) playing the "Dead March" in Saul; members of the St. George's Football Club Committee and players, who carried a magnificent wreath under glass dome, with inscription:

"In fond remembrance, from committee and members of St. George's F.C.;" deputation from Newport Football Club, bearing a very nice wreath as a "Tribute of respect, from Newport F.C.;" deputation from the Shifnal Football Club; then came the members of Snedshill U.M.F.C. Bible Class, with a beautiful wreath, "In loving memory of James Stanworth, from Adult Bible Class, Snedshill Sunday School;" several young men as bearers from the school, followed by Messrs. B. Griffiths, D. Lewis, A. Turley, James Barnsley, George Darrall, James Jenkins, H. Darrall' and J. Wallett; hearse containing the coffin (on which were placed several nice wreaths), the shield bearing the inscription, "James Stanworth, died April 25th, 1895, aged 26 years;" coach, containing members of the family.

Following was a large number of relatives, the teachers and scholars of the Snedshill United Methodist Free Church Sunday School, with Rev. J. Pearce (minister) and Mr. John Worrall (superintendent), the rear being brought up by the employees at Priorslee Furnaces. Arriving at the church gates, the Rev. J. P. Stephenson, vicar, officiated, and at the close of the lesson in church he spoke on the uncertainty of human life, and urged upon all present the necessity of living nearer to God.

The rev. gentleman concluded the service at the grave, when Rev. J. Pearce gave out the hymn, "We shall all meet at home in the morning," and then the procession reformed, the band playing the march, "The Vacant Chair," and thus were laid to rest the remains of one who was of a most genial disposition, loved and respected by all who knew him.

Employers also contributed something to the funeral, even if it was merely the permission for workers to have the day off to attend. When the death had been caused at work, the employer would usually pay for an expensive funeral and perhaps make a small gratuitous donation to the family, but there his obligations ended. No pensions or compensation were called for.

Both before and after the funeral, well-wishers might 'take a collection' between themselves and give it to the bereaved family. Sometimes the money would be used to purchase a 'decent' headstone, otherwise it would be used to help the family survive. It was as important to the lower classes as it was for others in society to provide a funeral tea, even if it consisted only of ham sandwiches and tea. Wherever possible, neighbours and friends would donate whatever the family could not afford, just to make sure that the deceased had a good and proper 'send off'.

Workhouse inmates, of course, suffered the indignity of a pauper burial when they died unless a benefactor was forthcoming. No trappings, no crowd to see them off, just a borrowed coffin and poor quality shroud. Death might make all men equal, but the journey to the final resting place emphasised the wide divisions which exist in life.

Finally, it is worth mentioning the funeral of William Ball, the 'Shropshire Giant'. About 5 foot 9 inches tall and weighing over 40 stone, the genial William was employed as a puddler for the Coalbrookdale Company at their Horsehay Works.

He died, aged 57, on 24 June 1852 and was buried in Doseley churchyard two days later, when crowds lined the road and filled the burial ground. It is said that it needed some twenty of his fellow workmen, with poles and straps, to carry his coffin.

Doseley church and (inset) 'Shropshire Giant' William Ball.

8

BURIAL GROUNDS

The burial of dead relatives, friends or local leaders in sacred ground is perhaps the oldest ritual performed by man. While the actual processes involved in the ritual have changed over the millennia, the end result is the same; a dead body is laid in the earth amid some sort of ceremony. What happens to the remains and 'soul' afterwards depends entirely upon the beliefs, whether religious or otherwise, of the society which conducted the ritual. In any event, committal to the earth is a common factor.

The part of the churchyard in which a corpse was buried was, traditionally, dependent upon the corpse or family's social standing. All bodies were to be interred with the corpse's feet pointing to the east, a remnant of earlier times when sun-worship was commonplace. Churches themselves were usually built with the altar at the eastern end of the building which was itself erected on a west-east axis.

Suicides had traditionally been buried in unconsecrated ground (often at crossroads) but most burial grounds reserved a small area specifically for them and another for infants who had died before baptism. Criminals executed at Shrewsbury Gaol could, until later in the century, expect their bodies to be given over to medical research; if they were lucky they would be interred in the prison cemetery.

The wealthier folk would usually be buried on the eastern or southern side of the church, the less wealthy on the western side (to catch the rays of the setting sun). The poorer classes, especially paupers and those who died in the workhouse, were buried on the colder northern edge of the churchyard, the latter in large pits which would be left open apart from a small scattering of soil over each shroud-clad corpse until the pit was completely full and another pauper burial pit dug nearby.

Churchyards were almost always typified by their air of peaceful neglect, where lop-sided gravestones and sunken memorials peered over long grass, rampant weeds and tangled briars. Self-seeded saplings and wild flowers intermingled with lichen-encrusted headstones whose weathering matched that of the church itself emphasised the lack of regular attention. As Dickens says in *The Uncommercial Traveller*, 'the grave-mounds lost their shape in the rains of a hundred years ago... contagion of slow ruin overhangs the place.' This image of neglect was the inspiration of poetry and 'Gothick' novels which proved so popular during Victorian times. Thomas Gray's *Elegy written in a Country Churchyard*, A. E. Housman's *God's Acre* and Bram Stoker's *Dracula* are but a few of the many literary works which romantically (or otherwise) exploited the mystery and decay of these erstwhile havens of tranquillity.

Yet it was not always so; churchyards were for many years a centre of local activity; fairs, games and other gatherings took place in them if there were no green or other suitable common meeting place available. During medieval times, for example, yew trees were the mainstay of weaponry for local retainers. Not only did they fashion their longbows from the branches of the churchyard yew but also sharpened their arrowheads on tombstones and carried out target practice within the confines of the burial boundary.

Indeed, yew trees were to be found in almost every churchyard throughout England; they were, since pre-Christian times, potent symbols of death itself and protected the living from evil spirits. However, they were also regarded as symbols of fertility, possibly because it was quite common for a seemingly dead yew to suddenly spring back into life, a new tree apparently regenerating from the hollow remains of the old.

Maintenance of churchyards has always been something of a haphazard affair. The church was frequently unwilling to pay well for the privilege of keeping grass and weeds under control. The job was often done reluctantly by the sexton or, more usually, by casual labour, whose scythes (themselves symbols of death) swished quietly in the still air of summer.

In many country churchyards – and it must be remembered that most churchyards in the Telford area were, in early Victorian times, adjacent to farmland and smallholdings – it was common for sheep and pigs to be allowed to roam freely between the gravestones in an effort to keep the grass short. While this was not a popular or satisfactory solution, it made economic sense, to the extent that the 1895 *Churchwarden's Guide* stated that there was no objection to sheep being pastured in churchyards.

Overcrowding in burial grounds was becoming, at the beginning of the nineteenth century, a very serious problem which was to get much worse as the century wore on. Its causes were attributable to three main factors; continued burials in a relatively small plot of ground over many centuries, the increasing popularity of headstones and a steady rise in the population.

The eighteenth century had seen a growing use amongst the working classes of the simple headstone; if their social betters could have headstones, why shouldn't they? This was bad enough, but the number of words they wished to have inscribed as a tribute to their dearly departed also increased and thus the general size of headstones was enlarged to accommodate them. The situation was exacerbated by the better off. Why should their graves be indistinguishable from those of ordinary folk? They, surely, must be honoured more ostentatiously.

As a consequence, the Church allowed the situation to get completely out of control as even larger and more outrageous monuments were erected over burial plots and vaults. The variety was limited only by their paying-power and lack of good taste; anything from large stone chests (empty, of course; the corpse must, by law, be laid in the ground) to tall iron railings around large stone or iron edifices which had an alarming tendency towards the vulgar. At first sight it is amazing that some of these monstrosities were allowed in the first place because a 'faculty' had to be obtained from the Church for the erection of any memorial which was not a normal headstone. However, it must be remembered that these wealthy personages would often be benefactors to the local church and refusal could cause offence – and a reduction in the amount of financial support.

The Church was almost powerless to prevent not only the building of such incongruous tributes but also the, by now, widespread use of coffins, particularly those which were made of stronger materials. Previously, most corpses were buried in their shrouds only. Decay was therefore relatively rapid and the same plot could be used for a subsequent burial after but a few generations.

Coffins took longer for themselves and their contents to decay. Lead-lined and 'air tight' coffins took even longer. Even a flat stone slab above the grave hindered the decomposition process. And large monuments were even more environmentally unfriendly because, once built, they made re-use of the ground almost impossible without some sort of conflict with the owning family.

Popular concern at grave-robbing, an activity which had been rife in some parts of Britain for many years and which culminated in the infamous Burke and Hare affair in the late 1820s, resulted in the Church having to permit the laying of stone slabs on top of graves and even to the erection of 'watch huts' within the churchyard, wherein the deceased's family sat and watched over the grave of their departed for several nights until the body was believed to have decomposed sufficiently to render it useless to a prospective anatomist. Robert Louis Stevenson's *The Body Snatchers*, written some fifty years after Burke's execution, revived those fears as did other tales of horror which proved to be strangely popular as literacy increased.

Charnel houses were also a common sight inside the churchyard boundary. Overcrowding was so great that the gravedigger could not help but unearth the bones of an earlier corpse. These bones were tossed into a charnel house – usually nothing more than a timber shed – where they would remain until a big pile of bones had accumulated and a large enough hole could be dug for them in this or a neighbouring churchyard, or a fire lit to cremate them. (The argument against cremations was a little weak in this respect; if it was unlawful to cremate a fresh corpse, why was it permissible to cremate the bones of an old one? Some cremations had taken place in some parts of the country from 1885 onwards, but the process was not legalised until 1902.) Although it was common belief that the gravedigger (often the church sexton) took to drink in a serious way to give him the courage to perform his ghastly duty, a fact which was exploited to great effect by Dickens in *The Story of the Goblins who stole a Sexton* from *The Pickwick Papers*. There is no doubt that sextons such as the Gabriel Grubb in the tale did exist; gravedigging was not the type of occupation entered into lightly, but at least the pay was adequate even if the work itself led to such men being ostracised by their peers. Gabriel's caustic but witty observations are well worth repeating:

> Brave lodgings for one, brave lodgings for one,
> A few feet of cold earth, when life is done;
> A stone at the head, a stone at the feet,
> A rich, juicy meal for the worms to eat;
> Rank grass over head, and damp day around,
> Brave lodgings for one, these, in holy ground!

The Towns Improvement Act of 1847 (enacted to reduce the spread of cholera and other diseases which were believed to emanate from poor sanitary conditions in towns and around churchyards) specified that there must be at least thirty inches of soil between the coffin lid and the surface of the ground.

Local regulations were able to dictate variations over this minimum stipulation so that three, four or even five feet of soil above the coffin lid were required. This did not help the gravedigger a great deal as he had to dig deeper. Nor did it remove the 'Problem of overcrowding; that could only be achieved by the provision of more burial grounds.

Several of the churchyards in the present Telford area may owe their origins to pagan or, more accurately, pre-Christian burial sites: Wellington's All Saints' parish church and Dawley's Holy Trinity church are believed by some to be situated in ancient cemeteries and it is possible that land adjacent to where St. Leonard's Priory at Wombridge once stood was also a place of early sacred significance. However, we have no proof and such assertions may simply be a case of wishful thinking.

These and a few other churches in the area had occupied their original sites for several centuries but had been rebuilt during the century before Queen Victoria ascended the throne.

✠ The church at Stirchley is thought to have been in existence since the thirteenth century, being a Chapel of Ease for Shifnal parish church. St. Mary and St. Leonard's church at Wombridge was erected on the site of an earlier church in 1757. It needed restoration in 1869.

✠ All Saints' parish church at Wellington had suffered damage during the Civil War and the present church was built in 1790, a few yards to the east of where the original church had stood. The southern edge of the churchyard was truncated during the late 1840s when a cutting was gouged out to create the new railway line and its attendant station.

✠ St. Michael's church at Madeley was rebuilt in 1797.

✠ St. Peter's church at Priorslee was built in 1836 to replace a much smaller and considerably older Chapel of Ease a few hundred yards away towards Shifnal, the parish it was built to serve.

✠ Holy Trinity church at Dawley had been in a sad state of repair for many years as a result of mining subsidence. It was demolished and the church rebuilt in 1845. The graveyard was extended in 1843 and again in 1890.

Apart from a few exceptions, such as St. Leonard's church at Malinslee (which was erected as a Chapel of Ease in 1805), most of the burial grounds in Telford were created and consecrated between the 1830s and 1850s.

This was the result of a national programme whereby the Church of England attempted to stay the progress of other, increasingly more popular, religions (particularly the various branches of Methodism and other Non-Conformist sects) by providing newer places of worship in closer proximity to the expanding centres of population. It was also partly instigated by the need for more burial grounds because the older churchyards were considered to be almost full.

Some of these were 'Chapels of Ease', churches which were built in parishes already with a church but which was too far away for its congregation to attend on a regular basis. St. Matthew's at Donnington Wood, for example, was built to serve the needs of those living in the Lilleshall Parish. Christ Church provided for the population in the southern part of Wellington.

The erection costs of these churches (and often a stipend for the incumbent) were frequently met by the more powerful landowners and industrialists of the time. One such was the Duke of Sutherland who owned vast tracts of land between Lilleshall and the present Telford Town Centre (constituting but a small part of his national estates) and was benefactor to several new churches, including that at Donnington Wood. Similarly, the Darby family funded the building of Holy Trinity church at Coalbrookdale and The Madeley Wood Company helped pay for St. Luke's church at Ironbridge.

New parishes were often carved out of those already in existence, much to the alarm of longer-established vicars who saw an unwelcome reduction in their annual incomes. Opposition and resentment amongst affected clergymen was mollified to some extent by the fact that these secular benefactors were both willing and able to provide finance to secure a living to those appointed to look after the spiritual needs of the folk in these newly defined areas. One of the new parishes was that of St. George's. St. George's church was built in 1806 but was not granted its own parish until 1861, securing land taken out of the control of neighbouring Lilleshall, Wrockwardine Wood and Shifnal parishes. The parish was originally known as 'Pain's Lane' until about 1915 when the name 'St. George's' was formally adopted.

It was undoubtedly a time of great change as the established church attempted to consolidate its position in a changing religious world. The new Church of England burial grounds created in the Telford area during this period were (with building or consecration dates):

Coalbrookdale	Holy Trinity	1851-54
Dawley	Holy Trinity	1845
Donnington Wood	St. Matthew	1845
Doseley	St. Luke	1845
Hadley	Holy Trinity	1856
Ironbridge	St. Luke	1845
Lawley	St. John the Evangelist	1865
Oakengates	Holy Trinity	1854
Priorslee	St. Peter	1836
Red Lake	St. Mary	1838
Wellington	Christ Church	1838

Very few churches which did not fall under the rule of the Church of England were permitted to perform burials. Exceptions during the Victorian years were the Catholics at Madeley (who were able to conduct their own interments from 1852 onwards), and the Society of Friends ('Quakers') at Coalbrookdale (whose burial ground was first used to inter the body of Abraham Darby II in 1763; the graveyard was extended in 1851.). Most of the Non-Conformist sects did not have 'proper' churches, but met in houses and other private buildings which did not have land attached suitable for burials. Consequently, deceased members of these faiths were usually buried in one of the Anglican churchyards. Anglican clergy in the area seem to have had good working relationships with the Non-Conformist ministers, and it was quite common for a vicar and (for example) a Methodist minister to officiate jointly at the funeral of a Non-Conformist.

The most short-lived burial ground in the area was that which lay in front of the Wesleyan Methodist chapel (sometimes referred to as the 'Central Hall') erected on the corner of St. John Street and New Street at Wellington in 1836. This ceased to be used after 1882 when a new Wesleyan chapel was built a few yards further down what was then New Street. By that time there were only six bodies buried in the small plot of ground fronting Central Hall; they remained there until about 1920 when the remains were exhumed and finally laid to rest in the town cemetery. Five of the bodies moved were those of Benjamin Smith, his wife and three of their children. Benjamin ran the town's first proper post office at 14 New Street and was father of the writer Hesba Stretton. He was also a leading Methodist lay preacher as well as a bookseller and printer.

The Burial Act of 1853 was passed as a result of excessive population growth during the first half of the nineteenth century; overcrowding in churchyards was a serious problem in many parts of the country to the extent that it was becoming difficult to find unused plots for new burials. Quite often the depth of ground above a previous interment was less than one or two feet and there were increasing grumbles that the stench of decomposition permeated the surrounding area and constituted a dangerous health hazard.

Recognising the difficulties associated with extending the amount of available ground for burial and the problems of a diverse and vociferous population who expressed a preference not to be buried in Anglican churchyards, the government had no option but to take steps to bow to increasing public pressure.

The Burial Act enabled local authorities to administer their own cemeteries, often sited some distance away from densely populated housing where its activities would not cause concern. Land shortage was no longer a problem and the charnel houses disappeared, to everyone's relief. In the Telford area, several Burial Boards were elected from the ratepayers in each local 'vestry' (an early form of local government usually administered by church representatives) to oversee the situation.

It was not until 1873 that the Wellington (Salop) Burial Board was in a position

Former Chad Valley Toy Works, New Street (now High Street), Wellington was originally an 1836 Wesleyan Methodist chapel. The curved frontage for the factory was added in the early 1920s on the site of a small graveyard in which Hesba Stretton's parents and three siblings were buried. Harry Corbett's glove puppet Sooty was made here and Kenneth Horne (of BBC Radio's *Round the Horne*) was a company director.

to purchase land off Haygate Road; it was consecrated as a cemetery in 1875 after considerable delay owing to a shortage of the Grinshill sandstone from which the original buildings were made.

By 1882 Anglican and Non-Conformist chapels had been erected in the cemetery. In 1894, representatives of the newly formed civic parish took over the cemetery's operation with the appointment of the Wellington (Salop) Joint Burial Committee.

The committee recognised that the grounds needed to be divided to accommodate the tastes and beliefs of all who would ultimately come to rest there. Separate areas were set aside for Catholics, Jews, Methodists and other Non-Conformists as well as regular Anglican or uncommitted folk. Land was also reserved for those unfortunate enough to die in the workhouse (now the Wrekin Hospital); their simple, often unmarked, graves ran alongside the hedge between the cemetery and workhouse grounds; a short distance from the death-bed to the cold, dank earth.

The Board also recognised the importance of advertising its existence and the rules under which the cemetery operated. This information appeared in *The Wellington Directory, Almanack and Diary for 1895*:

WELLINGTON
BURIAL BOARD

Rev. Josephus Judson (Chairman), Mr. Thomas Howes, Mr G. Jackson, Mr. A. Sharman, Mr.W. Smith, Mr. R. Jenkinson, Mr. W. Partridge, Mr. T. Reese, Mr. C.W. Hiatt (Clerk). Mr. J. Galbraith (Treasurer). Meetings are held at the Commissioners' Office, Walker street, on the first Tuesday in every other month, commencing in January.

CEMETERY
HAYGATE ROAD
ABSTRACT OF REGULATIONS

The portion of the ground lying between the Chapels and the Haygate Road, together with one of such Chapels, have been consecrated for burials according to the Established Church of Wellington Cemetery, England; and the ground lying between the Chapels and the Holyhead Turnpike road, together with the other Chapel are unconsecrated, any duly authorised or recognised Minister, Teacher, or Official of any Christian congregation may officiate therein.

A plan of the ground, showing the divisions into consecrated and unconsecrated portions, and the sections of the ground with the several Grave spaces thereon, is deposited, and may be seen at the Lodge, at the Burial Ground, free of charge, where also a Copy of Rules and Regulations and Table of Fees, and every other information may be obtained on application.

Notice of any intended interment shall be given at the Lodge to the Lodge keeper, between the hours of Nine a.m. and Seven p.m. on every day, 36 hours previous to an interment (except in special cases).

The notice shall be in the form provided by the Board, and the party making the application must be prepared with the Registrar's or Coroner's Certificate of Death, with information as to where the death occurred, the portion of the ground, whether consecrated or unconsecrated, and the section in which it is intended the burial shall take place, the name of the Minister to officiate, and the day and hour appointed for the intended burial; in the case of an infant, the size of the coffin, and in the case of a purchased vault or grave, the consent in writing of the owners to the interment. The proof of ownership to be in the discretion of the Board.

All funerals to take place in the afternoon between 1 and 5, except from the 29th of September to the 25th of March, when the hours shall be from 1 till 4, Parties must arrange for the attendance of the officiating minister, and to ensure punctuality, one shilling shall be paid as a fine to the officiating minister for every half-hour that he shall be kept waiting after the time fixed for the funeral. No burial shall take place before 1 or after 5 in the afternoon, except by special permission of the Chairman or Clerk to the Board.

All fees or charges, whether in case of common interment or on purchase, and whether payable to the Burial Board or to the officiating minister or clerk, in the consecrated ground, or to the officiating minister in the unconsecrated ground, shall be paid to the Lodge-keeper before the order for the burial shall be issued.

All vaults and graves will be sold subject to the present or any future regulations issued or to be issued with regard to Burial Grounds by a Secretary of State, the Burial Board, or other competent authority, and also subject to the fees payable or subsequent interments.

The selection of the grave space or spaces in all cases, both of general interment or of purchase, shall be subject to the approval of the Burial Board or Committee appointed by them, but the wishes of applicants will be met as far as practicable.

All grave stones, monuments, memorials and inscriptions shall be subject to the approval of the Burial Board, and a drawing, showing the form, materials and dimensions of every grave stone, monument or tomb proposed to be erected, together with a copy of the inscription intended to be cut thereon, must be left at the Office of the Clerk of the Board three clear days before such gravestone, monument or tomb shall be erected in the Cemetery.

A Certificate of the approval of the Board will be given before they can be erected in any part of the Cemetery. All questions as to the fitness of any monumental inscription in the consecrated part of the ground, are ultimately determined by the Bishop of the Diocese.

The burial ground will be open to the public daily from 7 o'clock a.m. till sunset. Children under 10 years of age will not be admitted, except under the care of a responsible person, and all visitors will be expected to keep on the roads and walks, and invariably to refrain from touching the shrubs or flowers, and to observe perfect decorum in all respects. Interments can take place on Sundays, between the hours of 1 and 4 o'clock.

The Lodge Keeper is authorised, with the sanction of the Chairman of the Board, to close the Cemetery against public admission, on the occasion of a Military Funeral, or whenever there is reason to apprehend from a large concourse of people, damage or disorder in the Cemetery.

W. TANNER, CEMETERY KEEPER

Rules is rules and (in theory, at least) they must not be broken even if you are wealthy. The problem with 'well organised' cemeteries is that they tend to be characterless, with more than a passing resemblance to a public park or garden rather than a respectful repository for the remains of our ancestors.

As the demand for 'respectable' headstones and other grave markers grew during the latter part of Queen Victoria's reign, so did the number of skilled monumentalists. Wellington attained the position of key player in providing a wide range of stone carving services. Having a respectable reputation for good service and reasonable prices (determined by the quality of stone or marble required, the degree of ornate decoration as well as the number of letters to be carved) guranteed ongoing success. Considerable pressure was exerted to ensure younger members of the family learned the trade to enable a business to continue for several generations.

9
MEMENTO MORI

Victorian England was probably the most productive and profitable period for stonemasons and monumentalists since medieval times. Not only was this a period of extensive public and private building activity but it was also an era when burial grounds were filled with monuments of all sizes, designs and inscriptions, as the chapter on Burial Grounds describes.

No longer were churchyards filled mainly with grass and weed infested hummocks; the need for a 'proper' headstone or memorial had by this time reached into almost every corner of society. While the law entitled everyone to have a grave marker, anything other than a simple headstone was supposed to have Church approval in the form of a 'faculty' – a dispensation granted at the discretion of the diocese.

Most of the stone used to create memorials came initially from the many stone pits and quarries in the area and were thus mainly of limestone and sandstone. Both are relatively easy to cut into shape and inscribe. Unfortunately, they are soft and suffer the effects of weathering, so unless inscriptions are deeply incised they are prone to be eradicated or rendered illegible quite quickly.

As the century wore on and transport of stone made easier by canals and the expansion of the railway network, harder material became more widely available. In some parts of the country, slate from Wales and Leicestershire increased in popularity because of its appearance and longevity, but in this part of Shropshire preference seems to have been given to granites and imported marbles (including alabaster) by those who could afford them. The rest of the population tended to continue to purchase local stone memorials which were, of course, much cheaper and did, after all, match the fabric of the church and would age in sympathy with it.

Not surprisingly, considering that the Telford area had a long history of ironworking, there are a few examples of cast iron memorials scattered around the burial grounds. These were invariably expensive to produce and consequently are not as common as might be thought. Apart from larger memorials, which might also incorporate a family vault, the most notable examples of iron memorials can be seen in St. Luke's churchyard at Dawley and at St. Michael's at Madeley. Both instances are mass graves of miners killed in two of the area's worst mining disasters which occurred in 1862 and 1864 respectively. Iron was much more likely to be used as railings surrounding the grave plot while the memorial itself would be made customarily of stone.

Traditionally, the stone masons who prepared, inscribed and were responsible for the erection of memorials in burial grounds worked at or in close proximity to a quarry. From the second half of the nineteenth century it was more common for them to have their own workshops (and 'showrooms') in the township.

Those working in the smaller settlements of the area were less likely to advertise their existence because their clients would invariably live in the same locality, but in Wellington, the main centre of population, there were several specialist monumental businesses whose advertisements in *Shropshire Trade Directories* (in many respects similar to today's *Yellow Pages*) were there to be read by a wider range of customers who could, if need be, take advantage of the facilities offered by the town's thriving railway junction to deliver memorials further afield.

A few monumentalist businesses survive for well over half a century, most notably the Lewis (below) and appropriately named Mort (above) families.

Some religious beliefs saw the headstone as a mark of vanity or arrogance; the Society of Friends, for example, had taken such a view but was obliged to revise its opinion because of the attitude of its members. Consequently, simple headstones recording nothing more than the deceased's name, the year or date of death and usually the age were permitted from the mid-eighteenth century.

There are a few exceptions to these rules, where a morsel of additional information has been added. These memorials, for example, are to be found in the Quaker Burial Ground at Coalbrookdale:

Samuel Rutter of Bristol 7.2.1845

Susanna Dickinson 12.6.1885 Died at Liverpool 9.6.1885 wife of Henry Dickinson

Charles Wilbraham died 1894, Aged 77.

Incidentally, there are several locally famous 'industrial' names to be found in this small burial ground, including those of Abraham Darby and Joseph Sankey.

There were several basic types of stone monumental designs which could be purchased depending on the ability to pay. Variations on those designs could be made, again at a price. Stone masons, like everyone else associated with the 'Dismal Trade', needed money to support their own families; they were not charities. Therefore, any design not in normal stock would be charged for depending on the amount of additional work involved.

Transportation and erection of the memorial were also items to be taken into account. The same applied to the inscription itself, which was cut into the stone with admirable skill. The number of letters, the size and depth of cut, patterns and motifs – everything affected the overall cost.

If the memorial was intended for a family vault, then successive charges could be made for dismantling the memorial (if necessary, depending on the design) in readiness for a subsequent interment, its re-erection and later inscriptions added to the original. While the memorial itself (once paid for) became the property of the family who paid for it, it was common practice that the monumental business which provided the memorial would be approached to conduct this work, assuming that the business was still in existence.

The most common monument was that of the simple headstone, essentially a large rectangle with an inscription on one side. (The practice of inscribing both sides of a headstone had largely died out before the end of the previous century.) Variations to this type of memorial mainly evolve around the shape at the top of the stone. The stone was erected at the head of the grave (hence the term 'headstone') and planted to a depth of about one foot; in most cases, this was sufficient to withstand high winds and the occasional sexton leaning against it in moments of contemplation or rest.

The second most common type of memorial was that of the cross, a single-cut stone inserted into a long brick-shaped base. The base bore the inscription. In fact, other shapes were produced and inserted into the same type of base unit (small urns, stone flower receptacles, etc.) although the cross was the most popular for several reasons: it was the symbol of the Christian faith, it was a straightforward shape for the mason to cut – and it was cheaper.

Kerbstone memorials were also popular. These took the form of a rectangular frame which encompassed the grave plot. The inscription usually ran along the inside edge of the kerb and a small stone vase, into which surviving relatives would place fresh flowers at regular intervals and invariably on the anniversary of the death, often sat inside the kerb at the head. Occasionally a small headstone would also be incorporated and small chippings placed on top of the exposed soil inside the kerb to keep weeds at bay.

Those wishing to attach more visual proof of their earthly importance chose much larger monuments to emphasise their relative positions in local society. Chest and table tombs satisfied this need. They consisted of a large slab supported on its sides by vertical slabs or pillars, the whole structure resting on the ground above the grave. Chest memorials were little more than an elaborate empty boxes (by law the body had to lie a minimum distance below the level of the soil). Inscriptions on table and chest memorials were cut into the uppermost slab; chest walls also had inscriptions cut into them, especially where the plot contained several related bodies.

Those who did not like the appearance of the chest or table opted for the pedestal type of memorial which gave noticeable importance to height instead of length. Urns, vases, crosses and angels with fingers pointing to Heaven were the popular emblems topping these constructions. Inscriptions were invariably placed on the sides of the more substantial stone blocks above the pedestal base.

Those with wealth sufficient to flaunt the fact of their existence and the importance of their family name in the local (or wider) community commissioned the design and erection of much more elaborate memorials. Two of the most notable which are still extant are the Corbett family vault in All Saints' parish church, Wellington and the Baldwin vault (see next page) at St. Michael's church, Madeley.

The Corbetts were an influential engineering family in Wellington whose agricultural implements in particular achieved world-wide fame. The memorial iron structure (see the photograph on page 32) originally lay in the churchyard in front of the western entrance to the church and was moved to its present site on the southern perimeter as part of the preparation of the present garden of rest in the early 1950s. (It was at this time that many of the still-intact headstones were placed around the churchyard perimeter and the remainder of the ground levelled for ease of maintenance.)

The Baldwins were important ironmasters during the late eighteenth and early nineteenth centuries. William Pearce Baldwin 'who departed this life Sept. 25th 1822 aged 68 years' was the first to be interred beneath the iron monument which stands on top of a brick base. Between then and November 1883 when his wife Ann died aged seventy-five, a further eight members of the family had died and were also placed inside the family vault.

Some memorials were little more than tokens of appreciation for or reflected the deemed worth of certain members of society, very often with close connections to the church inside whose environs these memorials (in the form of headstones in the churchyard or plaques, tablets (of alabaster, stone, marble or brass) and windows inside the church) were placed. Occasionally, items of church silverware, for use during communion, were donated.

The Baldwin vault in St. Michael's churchyard, Madeley.

Here are just a few examples:

From All Saints', Wellington:

> This monument was erected by public subscription as a tribute of respect to the
> memory of HELEN MARIA wife of the Revd BENJN BANNING MA Vicar of
> Wellington Rector of Eyton and Rural Dean. She departed this life March 9th 1877
> in the 62nd year of her age.
> 'Blessed are the dead which die in the Lord; even so
> saith the Spirit for they rest from their labour.'

> To the Glory of God in loving memory of JOHN CRUMP BOWRING
> of Bradley Moor, Wellington, who died May 18th 1894 Aged 59 years.
> The two windows 'Christ the Consoler of the Sick and Afflicted'
> 'Blessing Little Children' are erected by his widow.
> 'Blessed is he that considereth the poor. The Lord will deliver him in
> time of trouble. ' Psalm XLI v 1.

> In memory of HENRY STEVENTON of Wellington
> who was a member of the Choir of this Church for Thirty one years.
> Born May 4th 1860, Died September 24th 1897.
> This tablet is erected to his memory as a mark of esteem by his fellow Choristers.

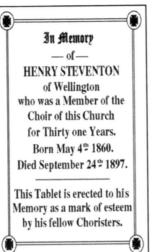

St. Peter's, Priorslee:

> Sacred to the memory of SAMUEL HORTON, Late of Priorslee Hall,
> Who died July 28th 1865 aged 70 years.

> In affectionate remembrance of JOHN HORTON (late of Priorslee Hall) Who died at
> Shrewsbury, January 19th 1863 in his 74th year and was interred at Shifnal.

And from St. Mary & St. Leonard, Wombridge:

> In memory of BROTHER THOMAS PAGE of Ketley Bank, who died
> February 10th 1882 Aged 53 years. This stone was erected as a tribute of respect
> by his Brother Foresters of Court Wrekin, Wellington. The deceased was also for
> many years sexton of this church and Superintendent of the Church Sunday School
> and in those offices served the Parish and his God both fully and well.

The more poignant memorials are those which reported the death of someone whose body, for one reason or another, could not be laid to rest in native soil. These are particularly sad simply because the bereaved families did not have a corpse to view and were denied that reconciliation deemed to be an essential part of the process which aids the acceptance of bereavement.

From St. Mary & St. Leonard, Wombridge:

> An affectionate remembrance of JAMES ALBERT SHEPHERD
> of the merchant ship "Duchess of Lancaster", who was washed overboard
> during a gale off Cape Horn, Lat. 48.00.S, Lon. 47.20.W
> on the night of the 1st July 1864. Aged 20 years.

To the remembrance of FRED SHEPHERD
son of John and Catherine Shepherd who perished in a snowstorm near
Cimarnon, United States of America March 1878. Aged 27 years. Interred at
Lake City, U.S. April 21st 1878. 'Faithful in life and pure in death.'

From All Saints', Wellington:

In loving memory of Captain St. JOHN MEYRICK MEYRICK,
Second son of Colonel SIR THOMAS CHARLTON MEYRICK, Bt. CB. of
Apley Castle. Born on the 4th of August 1866. He served for 12 years in the
Gordon Highlanders and was killed while gallantly leading his men against
the Boers in the South African war at Doornkop near Johannesburg on the
29th of May 1900. His body was conveyed to the Maraisburg Cemetery and
buried in the presence of his comrades and many kind friends 31st May.
'Well done, good and faithful servant, enter thou into the joy of the Lord.'

In memory of THOMAS ELCOCKS No. 4728 King's Shropshire Light
Infantry, son of THOMAS AND EMMA ELCOCKS of 17 Cemetery Road,
Wellington, who was killed in action in the Transvaal war at Lilliefontein on
Novr 6th 1900 Aged 25. This tablet is erected by his comrades.

Inscriptions required approval from the local incumbent, although it was almost
unheard of for any reasonable inscription to be refused. It was at this time that the
narrow-minded Victorian view of what was and what was not moral or dignified was
imposed. References to 'Dad', even if that was what 'Father' was known as to all his
family, were discouraged, a somewhat petty and trivial attitude which still prevails in
some parishes to this day. Instead, the Church seems to have encouraged the mass use
of trite phrases, misquoted sayings and pathetic poems whose use became sadly more
commonplace as the century wore on.

There were some vicars who recognised these trends but could do little to change
them, other than to observe them publicly if given the opportunity:

DECEMBER 1874
CEMETERY NOTES

After the services on my first day at the cemetery, I took an inventory of my new parish.
There is something grotesque as well as solemn in a public burying-ground. The grin of the
skeleton seems to lurk behind every grave. Death seems to laugh at its triumph over life.
On the tombstones were many holy texts, yet so oddly quoted, or so mixed with 'uncouth
rhymes', that their effect was the same as if they had been meant for a jest. The cemetery
had not been opened for more than twelve or thirteen years, yet in a brief walk of a few
minutes I found nearly twenty times the interminable

'Affliction sore long time I bore;
Physicians were in vain,' etc;

and so many were the various readings that the collection of them would have been
entertainment even for a Griesbach. On one stone at least I found the execrable doggerel:

'Pain was my portion, physic was my food.
Drugs was my devotion: but all was no good.'

The children were generally described as 'little angels'; and sometimes as 'good soldiers'; that had won a victory and were gone to another world to make a triumph. On one stone the philosophy of the death of children was explained at length. They come into the world unfledged angels, but as soon as their wings grow they take flight to a distant region. On another stone a disciple of Swedenborg had explained the whole mystery of the resurrection: the soul on passing from the body is at once clothed with a spiritual body, so that the body which has been buried is cast off for ever. It is said of a great many that their 'end was peace'. Many were described as 'husband kind, and father dear'; and not a few were 'respected by all who knew them'. Over the grave of a pious lady her husband had caused to be recorded, her 'life on earth was so near heaven, that when called hence she had but a little way to go.' There was only one inscription that seemed to have an intended levity. – *Recollections of a Cemetery Chaplain*, in *Sunday at Home*.

While it is a pity that such sentiments were expressed, the simple fact was that the bereaved felt an inherent need to record in some positive way the fact of the deceased's existence. A headstone was, to many (especially the less well-off), visual proof that those remaining alive had given the corpse a 'decent' burial, and a decent burial was what everyone desired when their time had come. Towards the end of the century there were still instances where families could not avoid the stigma of a pauper burial but whose friends clubbed together after the funeral had taken place in order that a respectable headstone could mark the final resting place. In cases of extreme misfortune, especially if the family's breadwinner died in tragic circumstances, it was not uncommon for a public subscription to be instigated not only to pay for the funeral and headstone but also to provide funds in aid of the deceased's family.

Not all memorials to the dead were oversized or full of hackneyed phrases, although a great many were. While economics might have affected the substance of a memorial it did not necessarily deny its existence; social attitudes dictated that a memorial stone must be supplied if one did not wish to be the subject of whispers and gossip, or be accused of being miserly or too poor or excessively frugal to do the 'decent thing'. How often are social pressures the root of hardship and hypocrisy! This was, and perhaps still is, why so many of the headstones in the Telford area record little more than the name, age and date of death of the deceased.

Nevertheless, the effect of religious beliefs and aspirations are very evident in inscriptions which go beyond name, age and date of death, and occasionally give some indication of the bereaved's thoughts on the Afterlife. These phrases occur in churchyards all over the area:

> Gone but not forgotten.
> Nearer, my God, to thee.
> The living know that they must die.
> He is not dead, but sleepeth.
> In God is my hope.
> Her end was peace.
> Blessed are the dead which die in the Lord.

Comments like 'He was respected by all' and 'His services to the community will be sadly missed' were generally confined to reports in the local press; it was not thought proper to put such sentiments on a headstone. Hints of sentimentality do appear in a great many inscriptions, for which Victorian attitudes are sometimes mocked and ridiculed. However these epitaphs are viewed by outsiders or observers from a different era, it is important to remember that they were written to satisfy human needs at a time of great personal distress.

'How sudden and how awful was the stroke By which the thread of human life was broke.
All mortal aid was vain my life to save,
So short the summons to the silent grave.
Reader, this case was mine, whoe'er you be;
Prepare yourself in time to follow me.'
'Boast not thyself of tomorrow,
For thou knowest not what a day may bring forth.'

Though long time afflicted and surely oppressed
Resign'd he endured it as all for the best.
Prais'd God for his goodness both present and past
And cheerfully yielded his spirit at last.

'If earth be filled with pain and woe, Weep not that I lie here.
If Heaven with love and rapture glow, Rejoice my soul is here.'

'A husband kind, a friend sincere, a tender father lieth here
This vale of tears he left behind, in hope eternal bliss to find. '

'One of the best of friends is dead, And they have laid him here.
Tread light upon his hallowed bed, For death has made it dear.'

'So lovely but so quickly gone, My memory clings to thee,
Thoughtless of death, the fatal blow Came suddenly to lay him low,
But, spared three hours, for mercy cried And at the feet of mercy died.'

'My flesh shall slumber in the ground Till the last trumpet's joyful sound; Then burst the chains with sweet surprise And in my Saviour's image rise.'

'Afflictions sore long time I bore, Physicians were in vain.
But death gave ease when God did please, and freed me from my pain.'

'An honest man of peaceful mind, a loving husband, father kind.
We mourn our loss, but 'tis in vain, We hope in Heaven to meet again.'

The list is seemingy endless.

Epitaphs containing additional information concerning the cause of death are extremely rare and are generally confined to tragic circumstances.

For example, a memorial to Captain Webb stands in High Street, Dawley (seen in its original location in the photograph below). This memorial is most unusual as the Telford area has never been noted for its civic tributes. Captain Matthew Webb was born in Dawley in 1848 and became the first person to swim across the English Channel (without using artificial aids) in August 1875. His subsequent legendary aquatic feats came to an end on 24 July 1883 when he failed in an attempt to swim across the Niagara Falls; his body was recovered four days later and is buried in the nearby Oakwood Cemetery.

In 1909, Webb's older brother Thomas unveiled the memorial which bears the inscription 'Nothing great is easy' in front of a crowd in excess of 1,000 people. It has since been moved to another part of the town.

None of us likes to think that our lives have been worthless or of no consequence. Even the simplest memorial stone is believed to bestow some degree of immortality on the most ordinary of lives.

Advertisement for Shillibeer's popular hearses.

Right: Monument in the graveyard at Christ Church, Wellington, to 20-year-old Thomas Bladen who 'Died from drowning through ice breaking while skating on Dothill Pool', January 1870.

Shropshire An _ _sition indented taken for Our Sovereign Lady the Queen at the House
(TO WIT.) of *James Wright* known by the sign of *The Park Inn* at *Wellington* in the Parish of *Wellington* in the County of Salop, on the *Thirteenth* day of *July* in the year of our Lord One Thousand Eight Hundred and Ninety *Two* before JOHN VERNON THOMAS LANDER, Esquire, one of the Coroners of our said Lady the Queen for the said County, on view of the body of *William Henry Edwards* now lying dead upon the Oaths of the several Jurors whose names are hereunder written and seals affixed, good and lawful men of the said County, duly chosen and who being now here duly sworn and charged to enquire for our said Lady the Queen when, how, and by what means the said *William Henry Edwards* came to his death, do upon their Oaths present and say that the said *William Henry Edwards on the Twelfth day of July One thousand eight hundred and Ninety Two at Wellington aforesaid was Accidentally Suffocated whilst in bed with its Mother.*

An inquest reveals the dangers of overcrowding, where children shared a bed with parents.

10

DEATH REAPS GRIMLY

It is unavoidable that the Grim Reaper will claim us all for his own sooner or later. Unless suicide is considered, none of us can tell when our last day will come. The majority of us, whether we like it or not, scarcely cause a ripple in society when we die, except to our relatives and close friends. Life goes on.

Whatever the cause of death, most of us are not important enough to warrant a newspaper report. No obituary is forthcoming; the best we can hope for is a simple announcement in the 'Deaths' section of the personal columns.

Nothing changes. The same was true for our Victorian ancestors. It is almost impossible to determine the full range of afflictions leading to death in the nineteenth century, nor the depth of feeling, hardship and misery that so many suffered during and after the loss of any member of the family.

Some causes of unexpected or untimely death are recorded, usually in inquest reports, and tend to fall into a small range of categories.

Infant mortality was high, although its rate reduced towards the end of the century. There are many instances of premature deaths of children for which silent and eroded testimony is witnessed on family gravestones throughout Telford. It was not uncommon for as many as seven or more children from the same family to die before their ages reached double figures. Poor sanitation and hygiene, lack of adequate or nourishing food, poverty, contagious diseases – all played their part at one time or another.

To lose a child through death is one of the most devastating experiences every parent dreads. If the parent happens to be single, the trauma can be even greater, especially as there may be no-one else to turn to for help or support. For a child to succumb to illness is bad enough, but when an infant dies for no obvious reason, the pain and anguish must be all the greater and can lead to the bereaved parents suffering an understandable feeling of guilt. 'Act of God' events, such as the seven-year-old boy struck down by lightning while playing with his iron hoop, were especially devastating. The best any coroner can do is to satisfy himself that a child died from natural causes, even if the precise cause cannot be determined:

OCTOBER 1840
WELLINGTON
PETTY SESSIONS

(Before St. John Charlton and T.E. Eyton, Esqrs.) Sarah Davies, of Daweley, single woman, was committed to the Assizes, for concealing the birth of her male child. The infant was found lying dead in a ditch, quite naked, on Wednesday last, and P.C. John Yates apprehended the prisoner at Ironbridge. When she was in custody she told Superintendent that she wished to tell him all about it; that the child was born on Sunday night at Forester's brick yard, and that she had afterwards conveyed it to where it was found. Dr Good, surgeon, at Ironbridge, stated that the child had breathed. Thomas Turner proved, having seen prisoner on Monday morning, at half past five o'clock, within about 100 yards of the spot where the body was found.

AUGUST 1885
MADELEY WOOD

FOUND DEAD. – An inquest was held on Monday afternoon at the Fox Inn, Madeley Wood, before Dr. G.A. Tailer, borough coroner, and a jury, of whom Mr. Perks was foreman, touching the death of Jane Parsons of Frog Meadow, Madeley Wood. – Mary Jane Parsons, the mother of the deceased, said the child died about five o'clock on Sunday morning. It was in its usual health until Friday evening, when she noticed that it was not well, but attributed this to teething. On Saturday the child became worse, but witness did not think it was so ill as to need a doctor. The child was very restless and witness walked about the bedroom with it until about four o'clock, when deceased became a little easier, and witness went to sleep, deceased lying across her breast. About twenty minutes past five her husband asked her how the child was, and on raising the child she found that it was dead.
– By the foreman: The deceased was in good health until Friday last. I did not think it was so ill, or I should have consulted a doctor. – By the Coroner: I had a child that died very suddenly in 1882, when it was two days older than the deceased. I do not know from what cause that Child died, as it was in its usual health the night that I retired to rest. The deceased was in an assurance society. I do not think that I shall receive any benefit as it had not been in three months. I have one child alive. I have had three children. – Matilda Pinchos and Jane Parsons having also given evidence, and the coroner having summed up, the jury returned a verdict of "Found dead."

AUGUST 1899
ST. GEORGE'S

SUDDEN DEATH. – On Saturday an inquest was held at St. George's, by Mr. J.V.T. Lander and a jury, on the body of George Fardy (15), a fitter's apprentice, living at the Rookery, who died suddenly on the previous Thursday evening. – The father of the deceased, William Fardy, a miner, said deceased had always been a delicate boy, but for the last three months he had been apprenticed to the Lilleshall Company in the fitting department. On the previous Thursday deceased returned from work in the evening, when he complained of headache, and lay down on the couch to rest. He was given some Epsom salts, and as he seemed to be in pain, was taken to bed. Dr. Wilkinson's assistant attended him, but the lad died the same night. – Dr. Wilkinson attributed death to apoplexy, and the jury returned a verdict in accordance with the medical evidence.

Poverty and destitution were also very common causes of death. Rather than allow themselves to fall into the unwelcome clutches of the workhouse, some people would travel long distances on foot in search of paid employment. In time, if a job was not forthcoming, the itinerant would starve himself in an effort to preserve what little money he still had; even this was preferable to entering the workhouse. In an increasingly weakened state he was unlikely to be fit enough to work even if he could find a vacancy. Finally, his health and strength would fail when he most needed them:

1843
SNEDSHILL

SUDDEN DEATH FROM DESTITUTION. – On Sunday morning, the body of a poor man, having the appearance of a bricklayer or labourer, travelling with a small bundle, was found lying near the brick works at Snedshill. Supposing that his inanimate appearance proceeded from cold, the persons who discovered the body carried it towards the warm kilns, but life was extinct. The body was subsequently removed to Shiffnal workhouse, prior to the enquiry of the coroner. It is said that he had some money in his pocket when found.

JANUARY 1848
WELLINGTON

CORONERS INQUEST. – An inquest was held on Saturday, the 22d inst. before J. Dicken, Esq. and a respectable jury, at Mr. Sandels's, Groom and Horses Inn, Walker Street, Wellington, on the body of Edward Blockley, a stonemason by trade, and a native of Bristol. Deceased was found in a weak and destitute state in the Church Yard, Wellington, on the 17th inst.: he was taken to the lock-up, where he remained all night, and in the morning was taken to the workhouse, where he died on the 22d. Verdict – 'Died from Natural Causes.'

It is an unhappy event when someone dies and even sadder when the name of the deceased is not known. Such things seldom happen today, when medical records and media appeals are often able to produce a name and relatives can be made aware of the situation. In Victorian times, such events seldom had a satisfactory ending because it was not often possible to let the bereaved know of their loss.

Death through excessive drinking was another common occurrence. There are many reports in the newspapers of men and women arrested for being highly intoxicated and spending a night or two in the local gaol.

Inebriation was particularly rife amongst the working classes, and who can blame them when they were forced to work long hours for meagre pay. Drink was a solace for many; it helped them forget their miserable existence, for a few hours at least. However, a drunk person is not totally in control of their actions. Fights and other acts of violence were commonplace, some resulting in charges of murder, a subject which is covered in the next chapter. Some would die from illnesses associated with continued alcohol abuse over many years. Others simply didn't know what they were doing or where they were going. Occasionally the discovery of a death caused by drink could be particularly harrowing to the person who found the body.

JULY 1862
OAKENGATES

CORONER'S INQUEST. – An inquest was held before H.D. Newill, Esq., coroner, at the Caledonia, in this place, on Monday evening, the 21st inst. on the body of a man named George Green, aged 21 years, who was found dead on the line of the Great Western Railway, on Sunday morning last. – William Oliver, the driver of a goods train, deposed: I was the driver of the goods train that left Wellington at 4.30 on Sunday morning; when I got near the goods station at Oakengates I observed something lying across the rails, which at first sight I took to be something that had blown off one of the waggons; I stopped the train and got down to remove it, when I discovered it was the body of a man; he was lying across the rails, and one of his feet was cut off; I aroused the station-master and we put him in the porters' room. – Benjamin Wright deposed that the deceased had been drinking with him on Saturday night, and that he left the house the worse for liquor. – It is supposed that the deceased, instead of going along the turnpike road, walked up the line as a nearer way home, and was killed by a passing train. The jury after hearing the evidence, returned the verdict of "Found dead."

December 1872
WELLINGTON

SUDDEN DEATH OF A WELLINGTON TRADESMAN. – On Wednesday last an inquest was held at the Raven Inn, Wellington, before J. Bidlake, Esq., on the body of Caleb Lewis, stonemason, aged fifty-three, of Foundry Lane, Wellington.

John Lewis, a son of the deceased, deposed that on Monday the latter left home to go to Prior's Lee about one o'clock; he had not been well for the last year or so, but it was six months since he had a doctor; he had hurt his leg and had a cold; did not see him alive after he left home. John Cotton, miner, of Snedshill, deposed to returning home on Monday night about half past eleven o'clock; he met the deceased walking home at Beveley; did not speak to him; had proceeded about one hundred yards when he heard some one call out, and he went back and saw Christopher Mansell with deceased trying to lift him up; he was not then quite dead; heard him breathe a little and groan; he died in about five minutes; Mansell left him with deceased while he (Mansell) went for a policeman.

– Christopher Mansell deposed that he resided at Beveley, and was returning home on Monday, about half past eleven, with John Ellis, when he heard a noise, and on looking round saw the deceased fall; went up to him and laid hold of him, but he was helpless and fell again to the ground; called after some people who were going up the road, when the last witness came up, and he (witness) went and fetched Police Constable Harris; had heard that the deceased had been drinking at Oakengates previously.

Police Sergeant Meredith said that he examined the body when it was being removed from the Compasses Inn, Beveley, to the house of the deceased at Wellington, and found no marks of violence on it. After a short summing up by the coroner an open verdict was returned.

August 1899
SUDDEN DEATH AT ST. GEORGE'S
A MORTUARY NEEDED.

On Tuesday morning an inquest was held at the George Hotel, St. George's, before Mr. Lander (coroner) and a jury, touching the death of William Overton (47), bricklayer, who had lived at Paget's Buildings. – Catherine Overton, the widow, said on Sunday night she, in company with the deceased, went to bed at 9.45.

Her husband then complained of feeling unwell, but she did not think much of this, because she knew he had been drinking, and he usually complained after a drinking bout. The next morning she saw he was dead. She had been told that deceased had been seen out of doors about five o'clock that morning, but if that was so, she was not aware what time deceased got up or when he returned to bed. Witness explained that she did not go to sleep until daylight, and then slept somewhat heavily.

– Dr. McCarthy stated that he was called in, but life was extinct. The surroundings were in a filthy condition. The cottage was very small, only two rooms, and everything about it dirty.

– Dr. J.R. Frost, assistant to the last witness, stated that he had made a post-mortem examination of the body, in a room in the George Hotel. The cause of death was syncope, probably brought about by heavy drinking.

– The jury returned a verdict in accordance with the medical evidence. – The coroner pointed out strongly the necessity of a mortuary being provided for the district. He said the house of the deceased was quite unfit for a post-mortem examination to be made, and there was absolutely nowhere to remove the body to for that purpose, had it not been for the kindness of Mr. Falshaw in providing a room at the George Hotel.

– The jury quite agreed with the coroner's remarks, and so members of the Urban Council being present, they undertook to bring matters before their council for consideration.

Traffic accidents happened all the time, most of which would result in a few days off work while recovering. Broken limbs and various minor injuries were to be expected, but sometimes the consequences were much worse. The majority of traffic accidents involved horse drawn carriages or 'traps'.

DECEMBER 1874
WELLINGTON FATAL ACCIDENT

– An inquest was held at the Oddfellows' Arms, High-street, Wellington, on Monday last, before R.D. Newill, Esq., coroner, on the body of Edmund Bladen, aged 50, a brickmaker and small shopkeeper, of High-street, who died through injuries sustained by a fall from a trap. It appears that on the Friday previous the deceased was returning from Dawley in a trap, in company with Mr. E. Shepherd, of the Wickets Inn, and a machine-man named Robert Jones, deceased occupying a seat on the dashboard. Between seven and eight o'clock on passing the Shropshire Brewery, the ironwork of the board on which the deceased was sitting gave way, and he was precipitated with great violence to the ground, dragging Mr. Shepherd with him. Jones was also thrown out of the trap. It was then discovered that the unfortunate man had sustained severe injuries to the upper part of the vertebrae, and that his head was badly cut and bruised. The poor fellow was at once conveyed home, where he was quickly attended by Dr. Brookes, who found the injuries to be of so serious a nature that he advised the relatives to call in the aid of a physician. Dr. Wood, of Shrewsbury, was then sent for, and on his arrival gave but slight hopes of recovery, and death resulted on the Sunday morning. The above facts were deposed to by Arthur Tyrer (a cooper of the Shropshire Brewery), Mr. E. Shepherd, and Robert Jones, who also stated that all were quite sober at the time of the occurrence. – The jury returned a verdict of "Accidental death." – Shepherd and Jones were also injured, the latter rather seriously.

JULY 1885
IRONBRIDGE

FATAL ACCIDENT An inquest was held on Wednesday at the Swan Inn, before Dr. Tailer, borough coroner, touching the death of John Delves, who met with an accident on June 18th, while riding on a break of a truck on the Coalbrookdale siding, which resulted in his death. – John Davies said he resided at Lightmoor, and was waggoner in the employ of the Coalbrookdale Company. He was engaged on the trucks between 10 and 11 on the morning of June 18th with the deceased. He was driving two horses, which were attached to a truck by the deceased. The truck was going from the station to the lower works down the main road. After the deceased had hooked the horses to the truck, he did not see him again until he called out. He drove the horses on until they came to the points. There was a truck on the coke siding, and as the truck passed the points, he heard the deceased shout. He said, 'Oh Lord, John, I am done.' Witness stopped the horses immediately, and went back to see what was the matter. He found the deceased lying in the middle of the fourfoot, and close to the points, and directly opposite the truck that was on the coke siding.

When witness went up to him he complained of great pain in his hips. – To the Coroner: I did not see any blood. He did not faint. He said he had forgotten that the truck was so near the points. I called a man named George Hatton to assist me. I did not carry him home, but I saw him taken home. The truck on the coke siding was placed there the previous day by the deceased's own instructions. It was placed there for convenience. Deceased did not usually ride on the side of the truck, but he did sometimes.

There was not sufficient space between the truck on the siding and the one crossing the points to allow a person to ride on the truck. – William Griffith said he remembered the 18th of June. The deceased was talking to him between ten and 11 in the morning. Deceased left him, and jumped upon the break of the truck to which the two horses the last witness was driving were hooked, and rode in the direction of the points. He did not notice anything more till he heard the deceased call out and upon looking in the direction of the shout, he saw the deceased lying in the fourfoot. He asked witness not to touch him when he went up to him. He complained of pain in the pit of his stomach and hips. He was quite sober. The horses were going at their usual rate. – Ann Delves, widow of the deceased, said that she remembered her husband being brought home about half-past ten on the 18th of June. He was immediately taken upstairs and put to bed. Dr. Proctor was sent for, who attended him up to the time of his death. Dr. Webb had also seen him.

Deceased remained in bed up to the time of his death, which took place on the 29th of June. – Dr. Proctor said he was sent for to attend the deceased about half-past eleven on the 18th of June. He examined him but found no external injuries. He was in great pain, and complained of his hips. Later on in the evening he showed symptoms of injury to the bladder. He went on well until the 27th of June, when he became much worse, and died on the following Monday. He had heard the evidence given, and he should say that the injuries he found, and what the deceased had died of, would be the result of a crash. The jury of whom Mr. W. Lewis was foreman, returned a verdict of 'Died from the effects of injuries accidentally received'.

November 1895
DECAPITATED ON THE RAILWAY
NEAR WELLINGTON

A shocking discovery was made near the Trench Crossing, Wellington, late on Tuesday night, the headless body of a man being found on the line. From inquiries made it transpired that the name of the deceased is William Shore, and he was employed as a platelayer on the London and North Western Railway Company's lines.

A son of the deceased, who is engaged as a porter at Hadley platform, appears to have left work after the 9.50 p.m. train from Stafford to Wellington had left the station, and after proceeding along the line for some distance he came upon the mutilated remains of his father, the head being picked up about a dozen yards from where the body was found. In addition to other injuries the two legs of the unfortunate individual were completely severed from the body. What brought the deceased on the line at that time of night appears to be a mystery, as he left his work at six o'clock in the evening. One reason assigned for his being on the railway property is that he would be able more readily to arrive at his home; but whether that is the case can only be conjectured. It is supposed that he was run over by the train which arrives at Hadley at 9.50. A widow and large family are left to mourn his loss. An inquest on the body was held on Thursday evening, before Mr. J.W. Littlewood, deputy coroner, when, after hearing the evidence, the jury returned a verdict of "Accidental death."

If death did not occur in the home it was more likely to happen at work, where conditions were distinctly unsafe for a variety of reasons.

Long working hours, poor diet, a tendency to drink and the employment of young children were undoubtedly some of the causes, but so were cramped working conditions and a severe lack of safety precautions. While most of the larger companies, for example the mines and engineering works, produced rules for the conduct of its employees, these were largely concerned with the need to keep production moving rather than to provide a safe workplace.

Even where strict procedural rules were laid down they were often ignored by workers who wanted or needed to cut corners in order to earn more money. Furthermore, they might not have been able to read. These were causes of several mining accidents, the subject of the final chapters in this book.

However, many industrial deaths were simply attributable to Fate assisting normally inanimate objects to deal the final blow.

September 1875
DONINGTON SERIOUS ACCIDENT

– On Monday morning last an accident of a rather serious character happened at Messrs. C. and H. Walker's Works, Donington. It appears that a young man named Waiter Hales was engaged in unloading some poles from a truck, and while being on one side the timber began to roll from the carriage. The unfortunate man had not time to get out of the way when two of the poles fell across him, causing such injuries that his life is despaired of.

November 1887
TRENCH

FATAL ACCIDENT AT THE SHROPSHIRE IRONWORKS. – On Thursday morning an accident occurred which proved fatal to a watchman employed by the above company, named John Haulston. While going round the works with a lighted torch he fell into a tank of oil, which caught fire, and he was burnt very badly. Dr. Jones was called in. The fire caught the building, and burnt it to the ground. Not all deaths were avoidable. Not all deaths were predictable. How many times have apparently healthy people just dropped down dead? Death may be a daily occurrence, but we can be taken completely unawares when the Grim Reaper's bony finger beckons and his scythe sweeps silently:

September 1862
KETLEY: AWFULLY SUDDEN DEATH

– On Thursday morning last, a young woman named Martha Harris, 19 years of age, came to the County Court office, in this town, to receive some money for her master, who resides at Ketley. She had just received the money from Mr. Gunton, the deputy registrar, when she suddenly fell, and instantly expired. Mr. Howlet, surgeon, was sent for, but on his arrival he pronounced that life was quite extinct, and that death had been caused by apoplexy. The body was afterwards removed to the Union-house, where an inquest was held the same day, and a verdict in accordance with the above facts returned.

OCTOBER 1865
OLD PARK

SUDDEN DEATH. – On Sunday last a man named Dunning, while about to rise from his bed to go to feed two horses, and while saying something to his children, was suddenly taken ill and died.

FEBRUARY 1885
MADELEY

INQUEST. – On Thursday, an inquest was held at the Royal Oak, before Mr. Deputy-coroner Potts, touching the death of an old woman named Susan Smith, of Station Road, Madeley. For the past fortnight the deceased had been confined to her bed, and on Monday night when her daughter, who is living with her, went to see her, she complained of being much worse. On the following morning she was found dead.

The jury, after a short consultation, returned a verdict of "Death from the visitation of God."

MARCH 1885
DAWLEY

PAINFULLY SUDDEN DEATH. – Great gloom was cast over this neighbourhood on Saturday last, through the sudden death of Mr. W. Tranter, of the Lord Hill. Mr Tranter, who had completed his 74th year on the Friday, was in his accustomed health, and attending to his duties up to the afternoon of Saturday, when standing with his hands on the table, he fell and suddenly expired. The members of Court 4430 of the A.O.F. (Ancient Order of Foresters), which holds its meetings at the Town Hall, on Saturday night expressed their sympathy with the relatives of the deceased, and unanimously resolved that a letter of condolence be sent to the family. Deceased was much respected in the neighbourhood. 'The Lord giveth, and the Lord taketh away.'

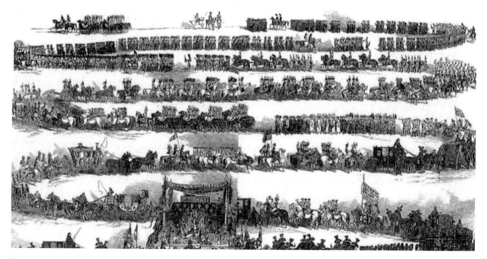

In 1852, a special excursion train was laid on to take members of the public from Shrewsbury and the (modern) Telford area to London to witness the state funeral of the Duke of Wellington. This contemporary sketch reveals to extraordinary length of the procession.

II

SUICIDE AND MURDER!

Who can tell what goes through a person's mind that makes them take their own life? Who knows what will be the final straw that drives someone to commit murder? Both suicide and murder are crimes. Although convicting a successful suicide is something of a waste of time as a punishment cannot be imposed, the local coroner still has to hold an inquest to determine the facts surrounding the event. An inquest also has to be held in cases of murder and, in normal circumstances, a trial will follow.

Suicides, in the majority of cases, are especially tragic; to contemplate the taking of one's own life implies a troubled mind and an absence of moral support from friends or relatives. Potential self-appointed victims did not have the benefit of the Samaritans or similar organisations from which to seek help. It did not help that many people in Victorian society regarded personal troubles as largely self-inflicted, yet those same people would be the first to extend sympathy to the consequent mourners. Fortunately, not everyone exercised a duplicity of standards or overt hypocrisy, but for whatever the reason suicides were not a rare occurrence.

These are but two examples of suicides reported at the time; hanging and throat-cutting appear to have been typical forms of escape.

FEBRUARY 1848
WELLINGTON

SUICIDE OF A HIGGLER: – An inquest was held at Mr Price's Queen's Head Inn, before Dicken, Esq. and a respectable jury, on Monday, this 7th inst. on the body of a man, name unknown, except that he was called George, who was found about half past six o'clock on Monday morning suspended to a beam, in the loft over the stable, at the above public house, quite dead. From the evidence of lames Cheese and John Crowder, it appeared that the deceased was a higgler, who travelled about with herrings and apples. He had left an horse and cart, with the name of Joseph Williams, fishmonger, Chester, on the cart, at Mr Price's, about a week ago, and had a quantity of apples in the cart.

He came to Price's on Sunday night, and asked for water; this was after ten o'clock; after he had drunk some water he went to bed about eleven o'clock; he appeared sober. After he had been in bed awhile, he complained of being cold, and got in the bed of witness Cheese, who is an apprentice to Mr Price. He arose about five o'clock, and at half past six o'clock was found by Crowder in the loft, in a sitting posture, with the halter tied around his neck, and the other end over the beam, which was only four feet above the ground. The end of the halter had caught in the nick of the beam. Assistance was procured, but he was found to be quite dead. No money, nor any property whatever, was found on the deceased, who was a stout athletic man, apparently about forty years of age. Verdict: "That the deceased hung himself with a halter, being at the time in a state of temporary insanity". Deceased had been drinking about the town the greater part of the week, instead of selling his apples. A person arrived at Mr Price's on Monday evening, and described himself as Joseph Williams, the owner of the horse and cart, and stated that the deceased was employed by him to sell apples, and ought to have returned to Leominster several days ago. He had heard at the Ironbridge of the deceased hanging himself, and from the sum of money he had when he started, he could not have much, if any, left. Superintendent Baxter, who attended the inquest, advised Mr Price not to give up the horse and cart until he (Mr Baxter) had received an answer to some inquiries he was making as to the real owner of the property, and that the person claiming it was the party he represented himself to be.

AUGUST 1885
DONNINGTON WOOD

SUICIDE. – An old man named Isaac Nicholas, who for the last few months had been living in a house by himself, cut his throat. The neighbours not seeing the shutters taken down, or the old man about, on Wednesday tried the door, but found it was locked. They brought the policeman, and he procured a ladder by which a young man went through the window, and he found the old man there quite dead. The house is some distance from any others. Much sympathy is expressed for the family and friends, as the old gentleman was widely known and greatly respected.

Fortunately, neither manslaughter nor murder occurred very often. Both tended to arise in situations where loss of temper got out of hand, but there were some instances where the prime motivation appears to be that of greed.

The murder at Redlake in 1812, the subject of the ballad composed in 1900 (see Chapter 3), was a case in point. The Stirchley Tragedy of 1846 may fit into this same category, although the motive behind the murder is not known with any degree of certainty. Theft was the most likely cause, but by whom?

The ballad of The Stirchley Tragedy (also in Chapter 3) gives some information concerning the background to the story, but then details the court appearances of the main suspect, George Harris. There is little doubt that public opinion was very much behind him, but the ballad stops short of giving the outcome of the trial at Shrewsbury Assizes.

The case against Harris was quite strong: he was caught in possession of several watches and chains – the victim, Barnatt Zusman, was a traveller for a Birmingham jeweller. Harris had been short of money, so how could he afford to buy such expensive items? It transpired that Harris had paid 10 shillings as a down-payment on a silver watch priced at £27 12s.

There was some doubt as to the exact time Zusman had been killed. Zusman had been seen alive during the afternoon before his death; Harris had a strong alibi for the evening. Witnesses say they had heard a gunshot at about six o'clock, and others had seen a nervous stranger (who spoke with a foreign accent) waiting for the evening train to Birmingham on the platform at Madeley Court Station. The stranger's clothes had recently been washed and he was carrying a bag. There were several other minor points which cast doubt on Harris's guilt. The trial lasted for longer than any other similar trial in living memory and the jury were out for almost two hours, a rare event in those days. The verdict of Not Guilty was welcomed by the Public Gallery and Harris was acquitted. It was thought more likely that the mysterious stranger was the guilty party: he was never caught.

Another 'murder' case – or so it appeared at first – was that concerning the death of Thomas Parton, a 65-year-old taxidermist of Wrekin Road, Wellington, who lived with his wife Emma and son Harry.

In 1885, neighbours heard a prolonged and noisy altercation emanating from the Partons' back bedroom. Shortly after midnight, Emma and Harry came out and told neighbours that the old man was dead, the result of a fall down the stairs.

The local doctor, Dr. Calwell, performed a post-mortem and deduced that Thomas had been clubbed to death with his son's walking stick. He also commented that he thought it unlikely that Harry had the strength to carry Thomas back upstairs to the bedroom without assistance.

Tongues began to wag; neighbours had seen Harry and Thomas fighting among the beans in the back garden. Thomas was thought by some to be drunk. Others denied this. Someone else had heard Thomas cry out, "Murder!" shortly before his demise was announced.

Harry was arrested with Emma as an accessory after the fact. She was soon discharged, there being insufficient evidence against her. At the trial, two senior surgeons disagreed with Dr. Calwell's opinion. They believed Thomas Parton's injuries were consistent with him having fallen downstairs and his death caused by the subsequent shock. They mentioned also that his brain had been affected by excessive drinking of alcohol.

Harry was found not guilty by the jury. There was loud clapping in the Court. Even though the verdict was in Harry's favour, was it correct? Only Emma and Harry knew. Acquittal implies innocence, but this is not always true.

Some investigations were quite conclusive, as this report illustrates:

COLLIER STABBED AT WELLINGTON
JANUARY 1848
THE LATE STABBING CASE AT WELLINGTON
COMMITTAL OF TAYLOR FOR WILFUL MURDER

Francis Cunningham, the Irishman who was stabbed in a conflict with some colliers on Christmas-eve, an account of which appeared in a former Journal, died on Wednesday last, the 12th inst from the wounds he received on that occasion. His recovery was considered doubtful from the first, although Mr. Steedman, surgeon, has been unremitting in his attention to the unfortunate man. An inquest was held on the body of the deceased on Friday, the 14th instant, at the Kings Head Inn, before Joseph Dicken, Esq. coroner, assisted by T. Smallwood, Esq. and a highly respectable jury, of which Mr. Whitfield, ironmonger was foreman.

George Taylor, a collier, who was taken into custody on the following day by the police, was present at the inquest. Mr. Charles Steedman appeared as his solicitor. A post mortem examination of the body was made by Mr. John Steedman, by order of the coroner and jury. The following is a summary of the evidence:

– The first witness called was Edward Owen, a Welshman who lodged with Cunningham, who, on being sworn, deposed that on Christmas-eve he missed Cunningham out of the house about ten minutes; heard a row in the street, and that a man was murdered; went out, and found Enoch Pritchard, a collier lying bleeding in the street; he appeared as if he had been struck with a poker; heard 'murder' cried a second time; saw a man running away, but could not swear to him; Honor Fynan, his landlady, cried out that Frank, meaning deceased, was murdered near the King's Head; found deceased lying on his right side, and my wife, Bridget Owen, leaning over him; deceased complained of his side; I then carried him to his lodgings;

was not aware at first that he had been stabbed; Mr. Steedman, surgeon, and Mr. Baxter, the superintendent, came soon after; deceased never left his bed till he died, on the 12th inst; deceased had been ill of the fever, but was got pretty well again; had been able to work a few days at draining; heard the name of Taylor called on the night in question by some parties who were running in the direction of Watling Street.

The clothes of the deceased, which were covered with blood and dirt, were produced; in the jacket was several stabs, and there were several more about the waistband of the trowsers.

Bridget Owen, wife of the last witness, deposed to the same facts as her husband; saw a man standing near to the deceased, with white trowsers, jacket, and cap on; a little further off stood another man, whom she took to be the prisoner Taylor, who ran away; there was a gas lamp near and she called out 'Taylor, I know and can swear to you'; cannot positively swear to Taylor as being the man, but to the best of my belief it was; had known Taylor before; some navvies were running after the colliers, and one of the navvies' faces was covered with blood; it was about half-past eleven at night when deceased was stabbed; my husband had had some drink, but was not drunk.

Honor Fynan examined – keep a lodging house, deceased lodged with me; there was a row in the street when deceased went out; when I went out deceased was standing near the lamp; saw a man cross over the road to deceased, and said to him 'You are an Irish b__d too', and then struck him; deceased cried out 'I have done nothing to you, boys' and made an attempt to return to his lodgings, when he was intercepted by the man who first struck him, and others also came up and assisted the latter to abuse the deceased; the man who first struck the deceased was dressed in white trowsers, spencer jacket, and cap; went for Owen, who lodged with her; deceased had only been out for a can of water, and as far as Pat Docherty's that day; he had not been drinking, as he had no money; there were about six colliers together with deceased when she went to help Owen.

Sarah Fieldhouse proved seeing Murrill go up to the deceased and saying 'Here is the Irishman'; deceased said he had done nothing to them, when Murrill struck him; several more came up and forced him down to the door, and all set on him; heard the blows; saw some of them given, as if a person was stabbing; there was a fight going on at Parker's beershop at the same time.

A boy named Jones, proved seeing the prisoner with a knife, which he described, and which was produced by Superintendent Baxter, and identified by Jones as the same knife; there was clotted blood on the knife.

The last witness's mother proved hearing a person sharpening a knife on her stone at the door, but could not swear it was the prisoner. George Murrill deposed to witnessing the prisoner, on the night in question, down on his knees, and working away with a knife as if stabbing; and saw his brother, Thomas Murrill, pull the prisoner by the collar off the deceased, and some of the navvies then came up, throwing stones, and forced them to retreat.

John Onions, of Ketley, proved being in Enoch Pritchard's house on the same morning the prisoner was taken into custody, and heard Taylor say that he had a row with the Irish, and that he had stabbed one of them. The deposition of Cunningham (the deceased) was read, in which he stated that he had no quarrel with anyone on the night in question, and took no part whatever in the rows going on. He went out of doors for a certain purpose, when he was attacked, as stated by the witnesses, and that he could not identify anyone.

Superintendent Baxter proved the apprehension of the prisoners, Taylor and Murrill. Murrill who had been liberated, was again taken into custody by order of the Coroner.

The jury having consulted together a short time, returned a verdict of 'Wilful Murder' against George Taylor and against Thomas Murrill, for 'aiding and abetting in the said murder'. They were committed, on the Coroner's warrant, and were conveyed to Shrewsbury Gaol on the following morning in the custody of Superintendent Baxter. Mr. Baxter has been indefatigable in getting up the case against the prisoners.

The final murder presented here was committed in the home. It has often been asserted that most murders are committed by a friend or relative. Remorse sometimes takes its hold on the murderer, who then commits suicide. The two events do not often occur within so short a space of time, nor does the murder victim usually succumb to death after the murderer has killed himself:

The Ironbridge Murder and Suicide
November 1887
SHOCKING TRAGEDY AT IRONBRIDGE
MURDER AND SUICIDE INQUESTS AND VERDICTS

Ironbridge and Madeley Wood were at an early hour on Saturday morning thrown into a state of great excitement on it becoming known that George Bouckley, 60 years of age, who had been very strange of late, had attempted to murder his wife, and had afterwards committed suicide. It appears that the old couple retired to rest as usual on Friday night, and between 12 and 1 o'clock the deceased got up and murderously assaulted his wife with a pick-axe. He immediately afterwards went downstairs, and was soon followed by his daughter, whose throat he threatened to cut if she interfered.

The wife then came downstairs, and Bouckley knocked her out into the street, at the same time throwing a hatchet at her, striking her on the head. The neighbours were soon alarmed and Mr. Smallman fetched P.C. Roberts, while another person went for Dr. Proctor, and during the absences of these persons Bouckley cut his throat and walked upstairs, where he was discovered lying on the bed, and within an hour died. The woman succumbed to her injuries on Monday evening.

On Monday evening, at the Golden Ball Dr. Tailer, borough coroner, held an inquiry on the body of George Bouckley, of Madeley Wood. … No sooner had the jury been sworn than the sad news was told that the poor woman whom Bouckley had attempted to murder had expired, and after some deliberation it was decided to go on with the inquiry.

– Annie Bouckley, daughter, who was accompanied in the room by Mrs. Lamb, gave the following evidence. Deceased was my father. My mother's name was Elizabeth, I have heard her called Wellings. We lived at Thave Street, and I remember Friday night very well. It was half-past nine when we all went to bed. I slept with my mother. My father was sober, and quite in his usual health. He had not been out that night, neither had he quarrelled with my mother, for they were good friends. I went to sleep very soon, and the next thing I remembered was my mother screaming. I got up, it was pitch dark, and found him, undressed, close to my mother, with a chopper in his hand, with which he struck her twice. He then ran downstairs, and I followed him, and he reached a razor from the shelf, and attempted to go up stairs, and I pulled him back, when he threatened to cut my throat. I loosed him, and went into the street, and shouted 'Murder' twice, and when I came back I found my mother on the doorstep and after he knocked her (the mother) into the street he threw a hatchet at her. I assisted her to a neighbour's doorstep, and did not go back till P.C. Roberts came. I never heard him threaten my mother that night, but he had often said he would put an end to her. They often quarrelled and fought. This happened about eight o'clock in the morning.

– Doctor Proctor deposed that he found Bouckley in the bedroom, in a sitting posture, supported by P.C. Roberts, who had hold of his shoulders. He was living, but fast sinking. He had a large wound in his throat, which was cut three separate times. The windpipe was divided. The cause of death was hemorrhage from the wound in his throat. He had been a collier, and broke his thigh. He stabbed his son some three weeks ago.

– Thomas Wood said he heard the daughter screaming 'Murder' at eight o'clock in the morning when he was working in his shop. He heard her say 'Will no one help my poor mother.' After that he heard her say 'You have killed my mother.' He was afraid to enter the house as deceased was a dangerous fellow, for he received some time ago from him a blow from a pickaxe.

– P.C. Roberts said in consequence of information he received he visited the house, and saw the woman covered with blood, and upstairs he found Bouckley on the bed, with a razor by his side, and a considerable quantity of blood in the bed. He sent for Dr. Proctor. He believed the woman was addicted to drink. – A verdict of 'felo de se' was returned. The jury was then re-sworn, and viewed the body of Elizabeth Wellings, who succumbed that afternoon.

– Annie Bouckley stated that when she got her mother into Mrs. Lamb's house she found that she was hurt in the head. She (the witness) was crying, and deceased said, 'Don't cry my child; I will forgive him, bad as it is.'

– Sarah Lamb stated that when she heard screams she opened her bedroom window, when Annie said, 'Sarah, do open your door, he has killed my mother.' She did so, and brought them both in. They had only one garment on. Deceased was streaming with blood, and she could only recognise her by one of her eyes. She asked her what he had done it for, and she replied 'I don't know, my wench.' She remained in her house till the day of her death. They constantly quarrelled, and only five days ago she had to shelter them. They were both 58 years old.

– A verdict of 'Wilful murder against Bouckley' was returned. – Strange to say some 16 years ago a Mrs. Harris committed suicide in the same house, which for several years, was tenantless, till Bouckley took it, and ended his days there. The locality has been thronged with people, who have a fancy to see the place where the horrible deed was committed.

Where a trial concluded with a verdict of Guilty against the suspect, imprisonment at Shrewsbury Gaol followed while the judge decided on the nature of punishment.

As the nineteenth century progressed, the number of crimes for which execution was the prescribed punishment was reduced. Furthermore, executions for those crimes for which death was the penalty were seldom carried out; sentences were commuted to life imprisonment or, more frequently, transportation to one of the British colonies for life or for a number of years.

Where the death sentence was pronounced, execution would follow as soon as possible. Last minute reprieves were rare. While waiting in his cell, the prisoner was separated from the other inmates. Being condemned to die brought with it certain privileges. According to the *Rules, Orders and Regulations of Shrewsbury Gaol, 1843*, he could expect to exercise in the adjacent courtyard every day leading up to the execution. Visiting rights were more flexible than for the other convicts. Condemned prisoners could be visited

'at all seasonable times, and at his own request by his Friends, one at a time, (except in the case of a child, or children with a parent), and no other person except the High Sheriff, Under Sheriff, Visiting Justice, the Governor, or other officer of the Prison in the course of his duty, and the Chaplain, (or if such convict shall be of a religious persuasion differing from that of the Established Church, a Minister of that persuasion attending at his request), and the

Surgeon of the Prison shall have access to such prisoner. Provided always that if any person shall make it appear to the Sheriff, or his Deputy, or to a visiting Justice that he has actual business to transact with such convict, or that it is desirable to obtain information from him respecting some Felony, anyone of these authorities may grant permission, in writing, to such Person to have a conference with the convict.'

However, the condemned man could be required to perform hard labour if the death sentence had been recorded at his trial but the actual pronouncement of execution not yet made, provided that his health would permit it. Hard labour might be stopped if the sentence was commuted to another punishment which did not include hard labour.

The condemned man's allowance ('Dietary No. 1') for daily dinner was different to that of the other prisoners. While for breakfast and supper he received the same as the other prisoners (one pint of cocoa or gruel in the morning and one pint of gruel during the evening), his dinner would be one pint of soup and one pound of potatoes, with four ounces of beef (cooked without bone) on alternate days. Women received half the amount of potatoes. The other inmates were served much less.

Meanwhile, while the victim awaited his last day on earth, carpenters were busy erecting a scaffold on the roof of the lodge outside the gaol. Each execution required its own scaffold; they were never used more than once. After 1868, executions took place inside the prison walls away from public eyes.

After sentence had been pronounced, the execution would be scheduled for the next morning provided it was not a Sunday. During the preceding night the condemned prisoner would be visited by his relatives for the last time, and the chaplain would talk to him, hoping to extract repentance, and while away the hours in prayer. At some stage the hangman would come to cast an experienced eye over the condemned man to assess his height and weight; these would determine the length of drop required for the rope to have its effect.

At the appointed hour, the prisoner was led from his cell to the scaffold, which was, by this time, surrounded by a mass of on-lookers. Children were pushed to the front, men and women crammed in behind. Everyone wanted a good view of the final act; executions were so rare that they must not be missed on any account. People travelled from miles around, even taking the day off work, to be present.

The condemned prisoner was made to stand on top of a trapdoor by the prison officers, who then tied the his hands behind his back and his legs tightly together. The hangman placed a noose over the head with the large knot carefully positioned under the left ear. After a last fleeting look at the crowd and perhaps a few words of contrition (quite a normal occurrence when faced with the prospect of an early meeting with one's Maker), the prisoner's head was hidden by a white bag hastily produced by the hangman.

The hangman would then wave the prison officers to stand back. The crowd stood silent. The hangman drew the trapdoor bolt and the prisoner was 'cast into eternity'. If the hangman had done his job well, death would be instantaneous; as soon as the body fell to the extent of the measured rope it jerked abruptly and broke the neck. A lingering death was the result of inefficiency. The body was then carried away either for burial or for medical research. Justice had been done. After a few moments reflection, the crowd dispersed.

The hangman, another job done, pays a visit to the nearest hostelry and sells the rope to the highest bidder, keeping the money by way of a bonus; the scaffold is dismantled. A new one will be built when the time comes.

12

MINING DEATHS

Of all the workplaces in the Telford area during the nineteenth century, the collieries and other mineral mines were by far the most dangerous. Hazards lurked in every corner of each and every pit and quarry; nowhere was safe.

A major cause of anxiety was that the mines, as a whole, were improperly managed. The owner of the land in which the pit had been sunk leased the mine to a chartermaster who had the power to hire and fire workers as he saw fit. Profit was to be made, often at the expense of proper safety precautions. Rules and regulations were increasingly imposed throughout the century, but still many shortcuts were made to maintain incomes. It did not help matters that even some of the chartermasters could not read or write.

The workforce was also at fault. Employees, too, were guilty of ignoring those safety measures which were supposed to be adhered to rigidly, as many an inquest proved. Furthermore, the employment of children (both boys and girls) in hazardous positions did nothing to help the situation. Even the women employed on the pit bank to recover small fragments of coal from the spoil removed from the pit itself were at risk.

Long working hours, improper supervision underground as well as on the surface, lack of care with important equipment and the maintenance of vital features – including the walls of the shaft itself – all were contributors to the rising death toll.

Natural phenomena were also waiting in every pit for an opportunity to claim yet another victim. Various inflammable and poisonous gases were, of course, an invisible hazard, especially after a pit had not been worked for several days as happened during the annual Wakes holidays. Water seepage was another problem and if the pumps had not operated for more than a day or two, flooding could occur. Collapse of the mine roof was another dreaded event; even mines where the roofs were not supported by sufficient pitprops were still kept open. Sabotage by nearby rival pits, where chains might be tampered with in an attempt to prevent coal extraction for a few days in order to gain an advantage, also occurred, sometimes with terrible results. Pit ponies, normally hard-working and placid in their gloomy surroundings, could cause injury and damage if they were startled and panicked. Coal trucks or sleds, often with no or inefficient brakes, were a frequent source of danger.

Profit was more important than safety, and men still needed a job to support their families. In short, no-one was safe if they had any connection with the deplorable activities entailed in working in a mine. That there were no more 'accidents' than actually occurred was something of a miracle, but a small consolation to those who did suffer severe injury or loss of family support through death. And it was not only the workforce themselves who were at risk; chartermasters also suffered by the cruel hand of Fate as did innocent onlookers.

Yet even with much evidence to show (at worst) malpractice and (at best) negligence on behalf of the chartermaster or an employee, leading to the death of another miner, criminal prosecutions were rare. An inquest's jury seldom found verdicts other than 'Accidental Death' in their repertoire. It was easier when much of the evidence was contradictory, as often happened where a witness was employed at the mine and did not wish to lose his job by testifying against his employer, however unsafe the pit might be. After all, he had his family, whether wife and children or aged parents, to support.

More often than not, newspapers reported the proceedings at inquests accurately, not afraid to pass subjective comments when they felt they were due, as the reports included in this and remaining chapters reflect.

NOVEMBER 1846
WELLINGTON

An inquest was held at the house of Mr. Hughes, Prior's Lee, by J. Dickin, Esq. coroner, on the 30th ult. on the body of John Bennett, a collier. It appeared that while deceased was descending a coal pit, with seven other colliers going to their work, a brick fell from one side of the pit, and struck the unfortunate man on the head, which fractured his skull, and from which injuries he died in the course of twelve hours afterwards. Verdict. – Accidental death.

JUNE 1862
MADELEY

CORONER'S INQUEST. On Thursday evening an inquest was held at the Miners' Arms, touching the death of a man named Kirkham, one of three who were burnt a few days previously by an explosion of gas at Halesfield pit. The inquest was held and a verdict of accidental death was returned.

FEBRUARY 1863
COALPIT BANK

INQUEST. – An inquest was held on the body of a lad, named Henry Morris, who died from the effects of injuries received on Thursday week at a coal-pit, which is managed by Mr. Enoch Evans, a chartermaster. From the evidence of the above named Enoch Evans and another witness, which was apparently reluctantly given, it appears that there is, in the said pit, at a distance of 25 yards from the bottom, an incline, down which the draughts of coal are let by a chain. It was the practice to hitch the chain to the draught (coal carriage) at the top of the incline while the carriage was in motion.

There was no stop-block to stop it in case of missing to hitch on the chain. On Thursday week there was a mis-hitching, and the result was that the draught ran loose down the incline, gaining velocity as it went, and struck the deceased, who was waiting for it at the foot of the incline. The poor lad died soon after being carried home … The coroner severely reproached Evans for his neglect, and stated that during his (the coroner's) experience he had found the chartermasters generally to be "the worst men who descend the pits," and as being "very indifferent to the safety of lives entrusted to their charge."

OCTOBER 1864
DONINGTON WOOD: SHOCKING AND FATAL ACCIDENT

On Thursday last an accident of a sad and fatal character happened at a pit at the Lodge-bank, at this place. It appears that the chartermasters had occasion to go down the pit some time in the afternoon, and one of them named Jackson left his daughter, a girl 20 years of age, standing on the bank. The two men arrived in safety at the bottom and were just going into the workings, when they were alarmed by the sound of a body falling behind them, and, on turning round they discovered the mangled body of the girl Jackson lying on the ground. It appeared that the girl had been leaning against a chain which fences the pit, when it gave way and precipitated her to the bottom of the shaft, a distance of 190 yards.

OCTOBER 1865
OLD PARK

FATAL ACCIDENT. – Yesterday week, at Old Park, a man was suffocated by what miners call "damp," or carburetted hydrogen gas; and another man was with some difficulty restored. – (On the subject of this accident we have received a letter signed "A Miner," remarking upon the frequent occurrence of accidents in the Old Park Colliery, which he attributes to the insufficient "timbering" of the pits. Is this the fault of the men, or the neglect of the proprietors to provide them with sufficient timber for the purpose? We think, with our correspondent, there must "be a fault somewhere.")

DECEMBER 1872
WOMBRIDGE: FATAL ACCIDENT IN A STONE PIT

On Monday an inquest was held at the Seven Stars Inn, Ketley, on the body of Thomas Birch, miner.

From the evidence of Benjamin Parton, miner, and William Guy, a chartermaster in partnership with Henry Birch, the father of the deceased, it appeared that the deceased, who was a holer was at work in a stone pit in the Wombridge field on Saturday morning, when two large pieces of yellowstone, weighing about four or five cwt. each, fell where the deceased was working; one of the pieces caught him on the side and the other on the hip, killing him on the spot. The roof had been examined, and deceased said that he was satisfied that it was safe, and the witness Guy had cautioned him to be careful. The trees (props) had been set close to one of the stones that fell, and were placed no more than two feet apart. Verdict, "Accidentally killed."

JUNE 1875
SHOCKING PIT ACCIDENT AT DONINGTON WOOD
THREE PERSONS KILLED

On Saturday afternoon, as the men were leaving work in one of the Lilleshall Company's stone pits, situated near the Lodge Furnaces, a sad accident occurred, which resulted in the death of three workmen. It appears that a blacksmith had descended the pit for the purpose of shoeing a horse, and some of the men were waiting to come up with him.

Three of them, anxious to get home, got into the chains (the usual mode of ascent) and gave the signal to be raised. This was done, but when near the surface, the chain broke and precipitated the three men to the bottom of the shaft, a distance of about 100 yards. Death was, of course, instantaneous. The names of the deceased are William Hall, a married man with a family: John Potter, 19 single; and William Johnson 16, single.

The scene of the accident was visited on Saturday evening and Sunday by large numbers of people. An inquest on the bodies of William Hall, and William Johnson was opened on Monday, at the Albion Inn, St. George's, before]. Bidlake, Esq.

DECEMBER 1875
OAKENGATES (PRIORSLEE)
FATAL PIT ACCIDENT

On Thursday last, R.D. Newill, Esq., held an inquest at the Caledonia Inn, on the body of Samuel Rushton, aged 16 years, who was drowned in the Woodhouse Pit, on the 7th inst. Mr. Wynne, Her Majesty's Government Inspector of Mines for the district, and Mr. C. Green, the Lilleshall Company's Engineer, were also present.

The following evidence was adduced: – Isaiah Holyhead deposed: I am banksman at the Woodhouse Pit. I was there on the 7th. I got there about five o'clock a.m. I saw deceased and four other men let down. John Williams was engineman. I gave the signal to the engineman. I had a signal up, and I signalled the engineman to stop. He pulled up. I knew they had been drawing water. We gave over drawing water at half-past two the previous day. Nothing was done to the sump before the men went down. I suppose it was my duty not to let the men go down till the sump was covered. I now know it was my duty; but I did not know it before. There are no rules in the cabin. The chartermaster was not at the pit.

– Isaiah Rhodes, reeve, stated: I went down with the men. I gave the signal to let down. The engine stopped a little where it ought to have, and then went on down just as I was stepping out into the inset. The bouke (bucket) turned over. The sump was not entirely covered. I saw deceased in the water, but I could not reach him. The water is about six yards deep. We got him out with a drag. He was dead. There was just room for the bouke to work when drawing water. We cover the sump over when we are winding dirt. It was my duty to see that the scaffold was on the sump. When I went down I knew the scaffold was not on the sump. It was safe if the engine had stopped in the right place. I got the three men out and endeavoured to rescue the deceased, but was not successful.

– Mr. Wynn: You are aware that they were drawing water the day before? – Yes. – And do you not know that it is your duty to go down first with one man and to see that the sump is properly covered over? – It had been the custom to all go down together, and I used to get out first and help the others out. – Are you not aware that the rule states that the personal safety of the men shall be your first care, and yet you allow this boy to go down under those

The Woodhouse Pit, Priorslee.

circumstances? – The 48th rule says that the hooker-on shall go down with the first hand. – Do you mean to say that deceased was the hooker-on? He was. – You ought to have gone down and covered over the sump. You would not attempt to draw stone with it uncovered, and yet you think it safe for the men.

– John Williams, engineman, said: I let the men down. Holyhead gave the signal. I let them down quietly. We had been drawing water the day before. I did not know how many were being let down. I knew the sump was uncovered. If I had known how many were going down I should not have lowered them till the sump was covered. I did not know that any more were going down than were necessary to cover the sump. The indicator has to be taken off the engine when winding water. I replaced it as carefully as I could on the morning of the accident. – Henry Tudor, foreman-sinker, deposed to finding the body, and to the state of the pit after the accident. – The Coroner then summed up the evidence, from which he inferred that there had evidently been a curious amount of neglect, and though not sufficient to justify a verdict of manslaughter, yet he had no doubt Mr. Wynn would take further steps in the case. – After some deliberation the jury returned the following verdict:– "That the deceased was drowned in the waters of the sump, and the jury are of opinion that great blame attaches to the banksman and reeve in allowing the men to descend without having taken the necessary precautions for covering the sump, which would have prevented the accident."

March 1885
KETLEYBANK THE FATAL ACCIDENT AT THE STAFFORD PIT

– On Monday an inquiry was held before the deputy coroner. Mr. Knowles, respecting the death of Benjamin Phillips, 16, employed at the Stafford Pit. – William Phillips identified the body as that of his brother. He worked with him at the Stafford Pit. – John Morris said he was employed at the pit to superintend the horse-drivers. On the morning of the 18th he was engaged laying a pair of rails on the down road. The deceased asked him if he might take the empties journey. Witness replied, 'Yes, if you like,' but told him not to bring back the tubs filled. The deceased was returning with the tubs filled, when he heard him shout his (witness's) name. Witness stopped the horse, and found the deceased lying across the rails quite dead. There was a wound on his head. His (witness's) opinion was that the lad was riding on the tubs, slipped off and caught his head against a tub. – One of he jury suggested that Morris should be censured.– Morris having been called in, the Coroner said the jury were of opinion that he (Morris) had been guilty of negligence of his own duty in permitting the deceased to do what he had done. He had been requested to caution him not to do anything of the kind in future. – Verdict 'Accidental death.'

June 1885
WROCKWARDINE WOOD

FUNERAL. – The funeral of the young man, Samuel Pickery, who was killed at the Granville (pit) took place at Donington Wood Church on Friday, and was largely attended, not only by his fellow workmen, but by a great number of the scholars and select class of Wrockwardine Wood. Primitive Methodist Sunday School, of which he was a scholar. The road to the church was lined with spectators, and the coffin and grave were literally strewn with wreaths and flowers. The burial service was conducted by the Rev. G. Todd. The young man was the only support of his father and mother, who have been ill for a long time, and for whom great sympathy is manifested.

Mining disasters, those instances where more than three or four people were killed in the same incident, were mercifully rare; only four major tragedies appear to have occurred during the Victorian period; each is the subject of its own chapter in this book.

Whatever gave rise to the cause of death passed into relative insignificance at the enormous personal suffering which followed each of these events. Tragedies such as these brought home not only the inevitability of death, but also its unpredictability.

Nothing can adequately prepare the human mind for death on so large a scale for such a small community. Perhaps our modern generation has become immune to the full implications of a high number of deaths occurring at one time; unless we are personally involved in a tragedy we cannot appreciate the full sense of hopelessness and despair which is a part of the experience.

The impact on the area in Victorian times was absolutely devastating. People came from all parts of the East Shropshire coalfield and beyond to see the site where death had dealt so cruel a blow. Despite the dangers, every able-bodied person in the neighbourhood did all they could to help: some risking life and limb to recover the bodies; others trying to comfort the bereaved; launching financial appeals to help pay for the burial and support the families afterwards. If ever there was a situation where a whole population could be affected by the cruel twist of Fate, the mining disaster inexorably brought everyone together in a common cause.

While there was an inevitable macabre interest in the scene of the disaster, the ensuing inquest and the funeral, the enormity of the event touched every heart.

After disasters such as these, the bodies of the deceased were supposed to be taken, whatever their state of completeness, to the nearest public house, where the landlord would set aside a room in which the bodies would be laid until after the inquest had finished. Occasionally, due to distress and confusion, the bodies would be carried to their respective homes and the coroner and jury would have the inconvenience of visiting each and every one before the investigation could be concluded.

In the meantime, funeral arrangements would be made – coffins produced, carriages and mutes hired, the vicar notified and sometimes the local brass band would be called out to provide suitable musical accompaniment to add a sombre note to the proceedings. In such circumstances, the pit owner or the owner of the land in which the pit had been sunk would meet all the funeral expenses and make a gift of money by way of compensation to the bereaved families. Considering their loss, the donations were hardly significant enough to support the families for very long, but at least it was a welcome gesture.

On the day or days of the funerals it was not uncommon for thousands of people from inside and outside the area to witness the melancholy event. Even with such large numbers, there was never any crowd trouble; everyone behaved in a respectful manner with due regard to the solemnity of the occasion. Sometimes memorial cards giving brief details of the event together with the names of the deceased were handed out to the attendees, including the family mourners. Before long there was likely to be yet another ballad sung in the public houses.

There is something to be said for communal mourning; while the bereaved family might feel utterly devastated by their loss, support from so many sympathisers must have helped them come to terms with the consequences. It made a dramatic and uplifting change to the moderately attended funerals of the majority of lesser mortals who died alone.

13

THE DARK LANE PIT DISASTER

The effect a disaster has on the local community is extremely difficult to assess. The very first disaster of its type cannot have been easy to come to terms with. The fact that this first disaster also happened to be the worst (in terms of lives lost) for the rest of the century serves to emphasise the enormity of the tragedy.

'Accidents' while mining in the East Shropshire coalfield may have been commonplace, with more than a few deaths, but there had never been so many killed in a single incident as there were at Dark Lane, a small settlement a few yards south of Priorslee, on 29 December 1862. Hitherto the sad record for single-incident deaths appears to have been three colliers killed in 1851 at The Rock, Ketley (as detailed in one of the ballads included in Chapter 3), possibly the result of sabotage.

The particulars of the Dark Lane Pit Disaster are gruesome. As the result of a vital piece of mechanism breaking, the cage containing twelve men and boys hurtled down the shaft, smashing the bodies to pieces.

The inquest held shows the pressures under which miners were put by their employers, and the lengths to which the employers went to prove that the cause of the accident had little or nothing to do with them. Despite the dangerous conditions in which they worked, the evidence of the men suggests that they were afraid to say too much in case their jobs afterwards were jeopardised.

These are the newspaper reports of the time:

DECEMBER 1862
PRIOR'S LEE
THE DREADFUL PIT ACCIDENT

We now give some further particulars and the evidence given at the Inquest. The scene of the accident was the No. 1 coal pit known as the Dark-Lane pit, belonging to the Lilleshall Company; it is situated near Prior's Lee, about a mile and a quarter from Oakengates, and two and a half miles from Shiffnal. The pit has been regularly at work for eleven years, and it is about 810 feet deep. From information gathered upon the spot, it appeared that about half-past five o'clock one "cage" of men had descended the pit in safety, and that at twenty minutes to six, the second set, which consisted of nine men and three boys, had taken their places in the cage. A rush is sometimes made by the men for places in going down, and on this occasion there were four above the number allowed by the colliery regulations of the company. The cage having been drawn up, it began to descend, and had only done so for ten yards, when the "spring-box" (by means of which the cage is attached to the rope) broke, causing it to pitch on one side, and fall, with the poor fellows, into the tremendous depth below. Shrieks of despair came from the doomed men, and mingled with the exclamations of horror and surprise of those on the bank; when, within a few seconds a low, deep crash issued from the shaft, telling those at the pit's mouth the fate of their fellow-workmen. It may be easily imagined that the men on the bank were for a time almost motionless with fright, while those who had previously descended returned to the bottom of the shaft and were nearly paralysed at finding the bodies of their companions, all quite dead, and in some instances literally dashed to pieces. Immediately fresh tackle was obtained, and one by one the mangled bodies brought up to the surface, but in some cases so dreadfully mutilated that they had to be recognised by their clothes rather than by their features. Great numbers had by this time arrived at the place, including the friends and relatives of the deceased; but it was not till all the pit's company had assembled, that it could for certainty be ascertained who were among the killed. A most singular circumstance connected with the accident was that the cage, which weighed about eleven cwt. after falling down and striking against the sides of the pit, became wedged in the shaft, at a distance of only eight feet from the bottom; had it fallen on to the men, there would have been far more difficulty in collecting the remains of the poor fellows.

The names of the deceased men and boys were: – John Guy (45), married, no children, Coal pit Bank; Benjamin Simpson (40), married, one child, Woodhouse Barracks; William Baker (35), married, two children, Oakengates; Thomas Tonks (30), married, two children, Sump, Oakengates; William Rushton (30), married, three children, Woodhouse Barracks; John Bailey (32), widower, three children, Roger's Row; Wm. Ferriday (37), married, six children, Prior's Lee; Samuel Jones (40), married, five children, Snedshill Wood; Wm. Hollyhead (40), married, five children, Snedshill Row; John Brown, aged 16, St. George's; Samuel Parton, aged 14, Coal pit Bank; James Smith, aged 16, Oakengates. By this lamentable accident eight poor women have been made widows, and thirty children orphans; three of the latter being left without either of their parents. The men were conveyed in carts (two at a time) to their respective homes.

THE INQUEST

On Wednesday forenoon an inquiry was opened at the Caledonian Hotel, Oakengates, touching the deaths of the unfortunate men above alluded to, before R.D. Newill, Esq. the coroner of the District. The following gentlemen composed the jury: – Messrs. J. Tarbett, Matthew Yardley, Richard Jones, E. Norton, J.W. Bourne, R. Millington, John Parkes, James Leeke, Henry Hayes, James Robinson, Thomas Morley, John Poultney, C. Edwards, John Parkes, jun. and W.P. Harley. Mr. Wynne, her Majesty's inspector of mines was present; as were Mr. T.E. Horton and Mr. E. Jones, as representative of the company. Captain Crampton was also in attendance during the whole of the proceedings on behalf of the chartermaster. The jury were sworn, and the coroner suggested that as the bodies were scattered about, they should view those of two of the deceased only, which were lying in the immediate neighbourhood. This the jury acquiesced in, and Mr. J. Tarbett having been chosen as foreman. Mr. Horton rose and said that before the proceedings commenced he should wish to express, on behalf of the company, their deep regret at the unfortunate accident which had now called them together. It was their wish that everything should be done that could render the lives of their workpeople safe, and nothing was further from their desire than any transgression of the rules. Mr. E. Jones said that everything that could be done for the relatives of the deceased in a pecuniary point of view would be attended to.

The first witness, a man named Noah Chirm, deposed: I was employed at the pit at which the accident occurred on Monday last; I am hooker-on at the bottom of the shaft; I went to work as usual on the morning of the accident, about 25 minutes past five o'clock; Richard

Richards is banksman at the pit, and was present; I went down in the first band, but I cannot say how many there were of us, but the band was full; the banksman gave the signal, "heave up;" he pulled the catch back, and we went safely to the bottom, the cage being immediately drawn up again; there were three persons then in the pit making preparations for the men to come to work; I was about commencing myself, when I felt the wind; at this time I was about 10 yards from the bottom of the shaft, but I knew that the men had fallen; I then went towards the spot, and found the deceased lying quite dead; the men afterwards came and assisted to get them up; it is a common practice at the pit for so many to go down; when eight have been in the band I have heard Howells call them in, and say there was plenty of room; this has been the case several times. A Juror: He did not wish to push them in, I suppose? Witness: He has called them. By Mr. Wynne; I have got a copy of the rules: it states that not more than eight shall go down in the band; I have not complained about it, neither have I heard anyone else: it is the foreman's duty to look after these things, not mine; there were three men in the workings, but not a reeve. Mr. Horton: They were firemen who had been down all night. Mr. Wynne: You say that it is the foreman's duty to make complaints, but how is it you allowed more to ascend? You were hooker-on at the bottom, you know. Witness: I have allowed eight to ascend, and sometimes nine; I know I am responsible, but I have not reported it to Ferriday; Howells and Richards had hold of each end of the bar.

By Mr. Bartlett: There were two fires burning upon the bank at the time of the men getting into the band, and Howells could see the number of men who go in. Examination continued: There was nothing said before the band was lowered, but I have heard the men complaining amongst themselves; it is hard work to keep them out of the band. By Mr. Wynne: The engineman would wait until he had my signal before he would draw up the cage. Mr. Wynne: Then you would have resisted the men getting in by refusing to give the signal? Witness: Yes, I could have done so.

Thomas Blower deposed: I am engineman at the pit; I went to work soon after five on Monday morning last; there were several of the men standing upon the bank; Howells and Richards were amongst them; it was about half past five when the first band started; Richards gave the signal, and I then lowered down; I cannot say how many were in the second band; Joseph Dabbs gave me the signal; I gave one stroke of the engine, which raised the cage, and I then reversed the engine; the cage went from the rope when it had descended about nine or ten yards; the men had never said anything to me about there being too many in the cage; Marrion has inspected the spring box, and the week before last he examined the rope and chains; I lowered the rope, and he examined it from end to end and also all the fastenings. Before the men went down I ran the band down at the one pit and up at the other; on the night previous I had also run them up and down; there was a good fire, and I saw Richards at the catch, and Howells going into the engine-house; when the second band went down Howells was in the cabin, I think.

Thomas Corbett deposed: I am employed at the pit in question; I went to work on Monday morning about half past five; I saw between 30 and 40 men standing on the bank; Howells and Richards were both present when the first band went down, but I cannot say how many men were in it; when the second band went down I had hold of the catch at one end, and Richards at the other; I do not know how many were in the second band; Howells would have seen to the catch if I had not been there; he was in the cabin at this time, but stood close to me when the first band went down; I did not hear the men complain on the morning in question, but I have heard them do so on previous occasions; when the second band was ready to be lowered a boy got into the cage, but was pushed out again; the deceased Guy would not let him remain. By Mr. Bartlett: the men were talking amongst themselves; they did not complain to Richards or Howells that I heard.

John Marrion deposed: I am inspector of machinery; it is my duty to examine the ropes and chains two or three times a week; on the 26th of December, between ten and eleven o'clock, I first looked at the rope at the barrel end, and I then examined the end of the rope at the pit; I also observed the chain, cage, and springbox; they were all right; during the time I was making the examination the engine went slower; the spring-box has been in use for about eighteen months; the blacksmiths put it on; when the spring is broken we can tell, and a new one is then substituted; I have examined the pins twice or three times during a week; I did so about a fortnight ago; I cannot say when the inside of the box was minutely examined; it might be three months since; when I looked at it, it was as good as when first put on; [the box was here produced.] The left side gave way first, but I did not observe any fracture when I last examined the box; if there had been I must have seen it; part of the box fell down the pit, and the other portion was left hanging to the rope; the box gave way at one corner and forced the other out; there are five other boxes of a similar description in use; there have been no complaints made to me; the engineman has told me about the men, but I told him not to let them down; I have received no written complaint; it is not in my department. Mr. Wynne: Before you retire allow me to tell you that whenever you see anything going on that you know is wrong, it is your duty to report it, whether in your department or not.

Mr. J. Lloyd deposed: I am engineer to the Lilleshall Company; I have examined the spring-box now produced, and supposing that there was no previous fracture it should have taken 22½ tons on the one side; it is 5½ inches by five-sixteenths in thickness; there is nothing to show the cause of the breakage; I am not aware that there was any more than the ordinary strains upon it. [The witness here quoted figures showing how he arrived at a knowledge of the strength of the iron]. As indicating good iron the fracture was a good one; the calculations are on a straight plate, but that ought not to make any difference when the iron is of good quality; the grain was in the length, and therefore in favour of the box; in bending the outer plate would break, while, perhaps, the inner one would be safe; Marrion ought to have seen it if there had been any previous fracture: he is under my control, and I have seen his reports of inspection; I have no reason to suppose that he had not made the inspection which he says he has.

Mr. E. Jones deposed; I am mining engineer to the Lilleshall Company; the shaft of the pit of the pit is 260 yards deep, and eight feet in diameter, and is fitted with guide rails; it has been worked very successfully for the last twelve years on the same principle; a wire-rope is used, and on an average one ton of coal is brought up at a time, exclusive of the weight of the carriage; the dirt brought up would probably weigh 25 cwt. and the weight of the deceased men would be about 15 cwt.; the box was one of Spence's patent; I have never had any complaints made to me, but about two months since I heard, casually, that a boy had gone down on the draught, and I was very angry about it, and told the men not to allow it again; rules have been distributed to all the men, and some time since all the bailiffs were brought together at the office, and particularly requested not to allow the rules to be transgressed; I was not aware that the rules are systematically broken; there are 48 men and eight boys employed at the pit.

Enos Pearce deposed: I went to work at the pit about half-past five on Monday morning last; the first band was not then gone down; Richards had hold of the catch on one side, but I cannot say who held the other; there were twelve men in the second band, and I tried to get in, but Simpson said "Get away, my lad, and go and fetch a rock wedge;" the cage was generally full when it went down, but I have seen as few as eight and nine; the previous morning we were talking about it at home; I never heard anyone complain of the number in; we cannot all go down in four bands; Richards gave the signal, and then drew back the catches; Howells was at this time standing in the cabin, but looking towards the pit; if he had liked he could have counted the men as they stood in the band; I am not aware that he did so. Mr. Wynne: Have you ever gone down with Howells yourself? Witness: No, sir.

Moses Lowe deposed: I work at the pit at which the accident happened; I have been employed during the last fourteen months, but have worked there some three or four years before; on Monday morning last I went to work as usual, and saw the first band go down; I cannot say how many were in, but there were about the usual number; I went to get in the second band, but seeing that there were already twelve in I would not enter; I said that I should not go down; Pearce got in, but was pushed out by Simpson. Mr. Wynne: Did he push the boy out because there was not room, or was it because he wanted him to get a rock wedge? Witness: Because there were twelve in, sir, and not room for any more. Witness continued: Richards and Corbett were at the catches, and the former gave the signal; I stood on the bank, and directly the band had gone out of sight I heard a crack, something like the cap of a gun being let off; Richards shouted "Hold," and I then heard a great noise in the shaft.

By Mr. Wynne: The men have complained about so many going down, but it has been amongst themselves; I have gone down with thirteen in the band; I never hardly go down with the first band, because I am afraid until they have been tried; I have seen Richards pull the boys out of the band, but he has never complained when eight have been in; the men were all talking about so many going down and riding upon the draught; I heard that some of them went to Mr. Jones about it, and we played the next day; after this there was an alteration for three or four days and only eight went down at a time; it only lasted for a few mornings, and then we got into the old habit again; the men who went to Mr. Jones were Daniel Humphreys and David North; I believe John Howells took no part in sending the men down; I never heard him call for more men when there were eight in the band; during the last fourteen months, with the exception of the days I have mentioned, ten or twelve men have been in the habit of going down in one band; I never went down with Howells, but I have seen him draw the catch when there have been eleven or twelve men in the cage.

Daniel Humphreys deposed: I work at the pit in question, and have been employed there about three years; I went to work on Monday morning last, about a quarter to six o'clock; there were twelve men in the band; I would not go down with that number. Mr. Wynne: Have you ever complained about the circumstances to the chartermaster? Witness: No, sir; but John Guy, one of those who were killed, has; he spoke to Henry Howells about it; the pit "played" for a day.

By Mr. Wynne: We could not all go down in four bands, and the engineman would not let us down after the draught was on; I and three others went to Mr. Jones about it; we met him in the road, and told him that the man would not let us down after the draught was on. Mr. Wynne: Then, in fact, you thought that if one rule had been broken, that was no reason why another should not be so too? Witness: Yes, sir. Mr. Jones: I understand you to say, then, that you did not complain to me about the number of men going down, but simply that the engineman would not let you down on the draught. Witness: Yes, that was it, sir.

Mr. Wynne: Then, it has been a regular thing, I suppose, for the men to ride upon the draughts. Witness: I have gone down with Henry Howells opposite the draught on the other pit, and I have gone down with Howells in the band when there have been eleven or twelve men in; Howells has said to the men, "Come on, there is plenty of room," when there have been eight in the band.

At this stage of the proceedings the Coroner said: Well. gentlemen, it appears that we have now arrived at a proper time to have the inquiry adjourned to some future day. It would not be proper, I think, to have the charter-master and the banksmen brought before us now, that must be at a future time. There will also be the evidence of Mr. Wynne, which will enable us to make further inquiries into the matter. The investigation is a most important one, as you must all be fully aware; and I therefore think you will not grudge the time spent in investigating this most unfortunate accident.

Some discussion then ensued, and it was finally arranged by the jury that the inquest should be re-opened on the 12th instant.

OF TWELVE PERSONS AT PRIOR'S LEE
CONCLUSION OF THE INQUEST

On Monday afternoon the inquest upon the bodies of the nine men and three boys, who were killed in the recent accident at the coal pit belonging to the Lilleshall Iron Company, at Prior's Lee, near Shiffnal, was resumed before Mr. R.D. Newill, Coroner, at the Caledonia Arms, Oaken Gates. Mr. T. Wynn, Government Inspector of Mines, and Mr. Edward Jones, one of the company's agents, were in attendance. Mr. Bartlett, solicitor, Wolverhampton, appeared to watch the proceedings on behalf of the charter-master and the banksman.

At the former inquiry the evidence given was to the effect that at half-past five o'clock on the morning of Monday, the 29th of December, a number of miners had assembled at the Dark Lane Pit to descend for their day's work. John Howells, the charter-master, and Richard Richards, the banksman, were present. A batch of twelve men and boys were lowered safely, and another twelve got into the cage. They had been lowered about ten yards when the spring box, which connected the cage with the rope, broke, and the cage with its living freight was precipitated to the bottom of the shaft, a depth of three hundred yards. The death of all these persons was instantaneous.

The witnesses who were examined at the former inquiry, could give no reason for the accident, but it was shown that an important rule under the colliery regulations, which limits the number of men descending in the cage to eight, had been systematically broken. The first lot who descended on the morning of the accident numbered twelve; the next batch, to whom the accident occurred, was of the same number. By this accident eight women have been made widows, and twenty-seven children fatherless.

The first witness examined was Mr. John Lloyd, engineer to the Lilleshall Company, who produced the box belonging to the drawing apparatus which gave way, and to which the accident was attributed. He stated that since the accident the box had been tested by hydraulic pressure, and had withstood a strain of thirty tons. He also made a statement, on the part of the makers of the box, to the effect that they had been makers of this description of boxes for a number of years, and that they were made of the best Low Moor iron. He had examined the box, and could see nothing to account for the accident.

By the Government Inspector: Patent safety cages had never been used in this neighbourhood; the objection to them was their complication, the extra weight, and the extra wear and tear; had seen Aytoun's and Callow's apparatuses, but objected to the number of levers and other complications, by which they were liable to get out of repair; had also seen Knowles's at work, and a model of Owens's apparatus; there was the same objection to all of them; the models acted well, but they failed when put in practice; if one of these safety cages had been used, and it had acted properly, it should have saved these men's lives; there could be no objection to the man Marrion ascertaining that the cages were in proper repair; there were four pits in the colliery having guides; he could not say whether the breakage would have been likely to occur if there had only been eight men in the cage instead of twelve.

Mr. T. Wynn, Government Inspector of Mines, was the next witness. He produced the rules for the management of the colliery, certified by himself and sanctioned by the Secretary of State. By the 24th rule the banksman is prohibited from sending down more than eight persons at a time. As regards the fracture, he could not give any precise information, but as far as his opinion went the fracture ought to have been seen by Marrion, if it had taken place previous to his examination on the Friday. The Coroner then summed up, and very carefully pointed out to the jury the evidence which affected the charter-master and the banksman, and the law of manslaughter. After deliberating about twenty minutes, the jury expressed a desire to hear the evidence of the charter-master.

John Howells was then sworn, and said he had been charter-master of the pit in question eleven or twelve years; Richards was the banksman; witness was at the pit on the morning of the accident; he did not see either the first or the second band go down; had seen the rules and read them; knew that the twenty-fourth rule stated that not more than eight persons should go down the pit at one time; could not say but that more than eight had gone down; had never received any complaints about the number of men going down; did not know that it was any part of his duty to examine the spring box; John Marrion used to do that. By the Inspector: He had not himself been down in the cage with more than eight men; there were twenty-nine men and fifteen boys employed at the pit; they went down in five bands; he had never tied them to four; he did not do so on the morning in question; he did not assist in sending them down either in the first or second band. This formed the whole evidence.

The jury then delivered their verdict, which was that of "Accidental death", accompanied by a presentment to the effect that, in their opinion, sufficient care had not been observed in examining the chains and machinery, and that the proprietors of collieries in the district should take better means for ascertaining that the colliery regulations are properly carried out.

Twelve people had died because corners had been cut and safety precautions ignored. There were no criminal charges brought as sufficient evidence was lacking. The men might grumble between themselves but they knew it was of little use complaining to their chartermaster, and the Lilleshall Company who leased the mines continued to turn a blind eye to the chartermaster's shortcomings.

The jury's closing remarks appeared to count for nothing. Human life was cheap.

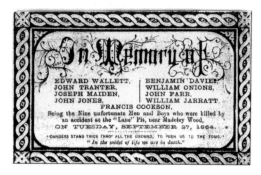

14

THE LANE PITS
DISASTER, MADELEY

There are only two communal graves in the Telford area in which are interred all the victims of a mining, or any other, disaster. One is at Holy Trinity church at Dawley, the final resting place of miners killed in the Springwell Pit tragedy of 1872. The other is at St. Michael's church in Madeley wherein lie the bodies of nine men and boys who fell to their deaths in one of the Lane Pits on 27th September 1864.

One of the victims was only twelve years old. One was thirteen. Two more were fourteen years old. While the remainder were adults, these four children must be regarded as sacrifices to the obscene nineteenth-century practices which permitted youngsters to work alongside men in the most dismal and dangerous of employments.

This was a particularly gruesome incident. The last band of workers were being drawn up the pit shaft after a long day's work. They were but a few feet away from the surface and safety when the 'doubles' or chains to which they were clinging became detached. Their screaming bodies plunged several hundred yards, smashing through a thick oak platform, into the watery sump below. The recovery party met with an awful sight; mutilated corpses floating in a pool of bloody water.

It presented the newspapers with one of those (fortunately) rare occasions when their reporters were permitted to express the full drama of the incident without holding back. This is the first of two reports on the Lane Pits Disaster:

OCTOBER 1864
FEARFUL COLLIERY ACCIDENT
NINE MEN AND BOYS KILLED

The inhabitants of Madeley, Ironbridge, and the surrounding neighbourhood were thrown into a state of great excitement on Tuesday evening last, by a report that a fearful accident had occurred at one of the pits worked by the Madeley-wood Company. Unfortunately the report proved to be too true.

The people of this locality are getting almost indifferent to the cry that another fellow-creature has been launched into eternity, so frequent are they of occurrence, but the fearful calamity of Tuesday created an unwonted excitement, and spread great consternation amongst them. The pit at which the unfortunate accident occurred is known as the "Lane Pit," and a numerous body of men are employed thereat. It is situate midway – or nearly so – between Madeley and Ironbridge, at a spot known as Madeley-wood, and is worked for the purpose of getting ironstone.

On Tuesday evening, about a quarter to six o'clock, the banksman received a signal that the last lot of men were coming up, and the engineman commenced winding. The poor fellows were ascending in what is commonly called the "doubles," that is in the chains, with a piece of iron over them (the bonnet) to prevent any falling stone hurting them. They were nearing the surface, probably not ten yards off, when the banksman spoke to one of the men (his father), and he made some answer. In a moment there was a sudden "click," and the chain losing the strain upon it swayed against each side of the shaft.

The poor fellow was horror-struck, for he well understood the sound, and in less than a minute his worst fears were confirmed by hearing a loud "thud" at the bottom of the shaft. To describe the scene that ensued would be almost impossible. The sound of the bodies falling attracted the attention of the engineman and some other employees of the pit, and being also heard in the road, the mouth of the shaft was quickly surrounded with a great crowd, who peered anxiously into the fatal darkness below. Some short time elapsed before anyone ventured to descend, but at length a party of miners volunteered to search for the bodies.

Such consternation was created among the men that it was almost impossible to ascertain the real number of poor fellows below, and it was feared at one time that the calamity would prove of a still more serious character.

The pit, we were informed, is something like 250 yards deep, and within a few yards of the bottom a scaffolding was erected on which the deceased worked in getting the stone. This scaffolding consisted of uprights, with oak planks thrown across six inches in thickness.

In the space under this (the sump) the water accumulated. The band of explorers having descended, stopped at the scaffold, which they found had been broken through by the weight of the falling bodies. No sight of the remains of the poor fellows was yet obtained. Descending lower, however, the men looked eagerly at the water, and sickened at the sight, for it had already become the colour of blood. And they knew too well the cause. Some of the poor fellows were totally unmanned, and were obliged to be taken to bank. And no wonder that it was so, for a more ghastly picture it is almost impossible to imagine. The little band of explorers gazing into each other's faces, white with a deadly fear, fearful and yet anxious to commence their trying task the hoarse shouting of the people on the bank – the wailing cry of distress which reverberated with an unearthly sound above, below, and around them – that agonising cry which told of a mother's grief and a wife's despair – were the accompaniments of a tableau already fearful in its scenic effects. Almost mechanically the poor fellows commenced searching for the remains of their unfortunate companions, and as each well-remembered form, crushed and mangled as it was, was drawn out of the water the poor fellows shuddered at the wreck before them.

St. Michael's church, Madeley, designed by Thomas Telford and erected in 1797, and the communal grave of the nine miners killed in the Lane Pits Disaster.

The features of some of the corpses were nearly unrecognisable, but others appeared with a smile upon their countenances, although crushed and mangled in other parts of their bodies. Such was the picture-calculated to appal even the strongest heart. One by one the bodies were sent to bank, and as quickly as possible conveyed to a public-house near, to await the coroner's inquest.

As the last body was brought to bank the crowd began to disperse, a settled gloom spreading over the whole neighbourhood. The accident was caused, it is believed, by the insecure manner in which the doubles were fastened to the chain. We say – believed, because it can never be rightly known, inasmuch as not one of the unfortunate creatures is left alive to tell the tale.

The doubles hook on to the winding chain, the former being protected with an iron shield or bonnet. Both hooks are still perfectly sound, and the hypothesis is, therefore, that the one hook, instead of being properly placed over the other, merely rested on the point, and the poor fellows probably moving caused it to slip off, and so hurried them into eternity.

Those who could possibly have been blamed have perished through their own carelessness. We append the list of the killed:

MEN

Edward Wallace, 52, married, four children, Madeley-wood Green. Benjamin Davies, 35, single, Madeleywood Green. John Tranter, 37, married, five children, Madeley-wood Green.

BOYS

William Onions, 12, Madeley-wood Green. Joseph Maiden, 18, Madeley-wood Green. John Farr, 14, Lincoln-hill. John Jones, 14, Madeley-wood Green. William Jarrat, 18, Madeley-wood Green. Francis Cookson, 13, Park-lane.

At the public-house to which the bodies were taken, they were laid out on the floor of one of the rooms, and covered with sheets. Until a late hour of the night of Tuesday the house was besieged with an anxious crowd – men, women, and children, striving to get a sight of the mangled bodies within. On Wednesday morning and, indeed, throughout the whole of the day, the same thing occurred. So great was the pressure of the crowd that the doors of the house had to be locked, but even this was not sufficient, for some persons obtained ingress at the back of the premises, and crowded into the room in which the bodies were laid, and great difficulty was experienced in getting them out. The relatives of the deceased men were allowed admittance, after the jury had inspected the bodies. The room door was guarded by a workman – an intelligent young fellow – and while our reporter was standing in the house the applications for admittance were very frequent, but had to be met with a refusal. In one case a man begged hard to be admitted, but he was answered in a tone of entreaty, "You canna come in lad – do keep back." In reply the poor fellow (we understood he was a brother to one of the men killed) pressed into the hand of the door keeper a clean shirt, and as the tears ran down his cheeks, said, in a broken-hearted tone, "Put it on him; it will make him clean and decent." Such scenes as this, we were told, were of frequent occurrence.

The second newspaper report, again presented with more than a hint of drama intended to emphasise the essentially human aspect of the affair, was as follows:

October 1864
APPALLING ACCIDENT AT THE LANE PITS: NINE LIVES LOST

On Tuesday evening last the inhabitants of Madeley, Madeley Wood, and Ironbridge, were startled by the news that nine men and boys had been suddenly plunged into eternity by falling down one of the Lane pits, situate about half way between the above towns. It appears that about six o'clock on the afternoon of the above day the last band of men and boys were ascending the shaft after completing their day's work, and that when about 300 or 400 feet from the bottom the doubles, or chains, in which the workmen ascend or descend the shaft, suddenly became detached, and the whole were dashed to the bottom. The force of the fall, accelerated by the doubles and iron bonnet, both together about 5 cwt. was such that the wooden platform of six inch planks was broken through, and the sound of the concussion was heard by persons passing along the road.

The news of the catastrophe spread like wild fire, and men, women, and children, pale with fright, and fearing the worst, ran screaming and crying to the pit's mouth, where hundreds were soon congregated. Volunteers, men accustomed to such scenes – fortunately, however, not often on so large a scale – came forward to descend the shaft in search of the poor fellows, of whose fate those conversant with deep mining could entertain but little doubt. Night set in, and mothers, wives, and daughters were led reluctantly away, but by the feeble light of a number of pit candles one distinguished a host of gloomy faces, still from which all hopes had fled, crowded round the mouth of the shaft, while amidst the hushed and silent crowd anxious questions were now and then addressed to the men who had descended the pit, and who in a few emphatic words described the scene below.

Indeed, even to their stout hearts a contemplation of what met the eye was appalling; men and boys in a torn and mangled mass were found to have been thrust through the platform from which the mine is worked into the sump, or bottom of the shaft, the water in which was discoloured by their blood, and bags were called for to conceal deformities the cause of death had made, before sending the bodies to the top, where a mournful anxiety was evinced as one after another of the victims was received and deposited in carts waiting to receive them, and to take them to a large room at the George and Dragon public house, Madeley Wood, where it was thought advisable to wash and prepare the bodies before submitting them for the inspection and recognition of their friends. The accident has cast a gloom over the entire neighbourhood, and it is highly creditable to the Madeley Wood Company, in whose field the accident happened, that they have done what they could to mitigate the sorrows of the relatives, by visiting them, consoling with them, and sending substantial relief. They also took upon themselves the expenses of the funeral, providing coffins, hearses, &c.

As usual, an inquest was held as soon as possible after the event, not only to ascertain the cause of death to satisfy the legal requirements but also to allow the bodies to be interred without undue delay. The verdict was the expected 'Accidental death' and in this instance seems to have been justified. While many 'accidents' were, in reality, nothing less than human error or incompetence, here the hand of Fate appears to have made its mark with a vengeance.

THE INQUEST

An inquest was held before E.G. Bartlam, Esq. coroner, and the following jury, at the George and Dragon, Madeley Wood, at 4 p.m. on Wednesday : – Messrs. E. Dixon, E. Harris, Edward Harris, Edward Smith, Wm. Price, C. Harvey, Thomas Price, S.H. Mangham, Thomas Price, Henry Storey, Thos. Franks, T.J. Boycott, and Thomas Instone.

The first witness called was Joseph Vaughan, engine driver, who having been sworn, said he lived in the parish of Madeley, and that he drove an engine for the Madeley Wood Company at a pit called the Brickkiln Leasow, or Lane Pit; on the 27th of September he was at work;

he was employed on that day to draw up the men and boys whose names had been read over; he had the signal to pull up a band of men at twenty minutes to six; he started the engine, and when the men were half-way up the pit, which was 240 yards deep, he felt the weight go off the engine; he had the engine handle in his hand at the time; he immediately looked at the indicator, and remarked to himself 'Oh dear, they were half way up, and are dashed to pieces', and then he stopped the engine, and went to the pit's head.

William Wallet, banksman, the next witness called, said on the 27th day of September he was at work on the bank of a store pit, called the Lane Pit, belonging to the Madeley Wood Company; the doubles were kept down at the bottom of the pit; the parties went down by them in the morning, and in the evening, between five and six o'clock, he had the signal that the men wished to come up the pit; he was at the back of the pit at the time, as he always was when men were coming up; the first thing he saw was the chain swinging; he then heard the bonnet strike the side of the shaft; he also heard one scream and found that they were gone to the bottom; he then thought he heard the men at the bottom lift the bonnet from over them, but he now thought it must have been the scaffolding at the bottom giving way.

Joseph Morris said he worked at the Lane pits, and that he was at work there on the day of the accident, at an adjoining pit, where they got pennystone; he came up at five o'clock at night, with six others; he went home, and being told of the accident at the other pit, he ran up; lames Davies asked witness if he would go down, and he did so with two others; when they got to the bottom they found the scaffold over the sump broken through; they then called for the band to be pulled up, and there came three other men down; there was water in the sump, he should think about twelve feet, and they could not see the bodies; they procured a drag, and got up the bodies of the three men and six boys; they were all dead, and mutilated; the scaffolding was very strong.

– In reply to Mr. Wynn, witness said they found the doubles and bonnet in the sump just as they now were; the bearers of the scaffold were broken; he saw the doubles brought up out of the water to the inset; every thing but the scaffold was unbroken; he considered the hook of the double to be in a proper working state; he could not account for the accident, unless that the link was not properly put onto the hook; he had not heard, nor did he know, of six men having come up six months ago in the same way.

– In reply to Mr. John Anstice, witness said he only saw one bearer broken; the bonnet was neither bent nor broken; it was then in the same state as now. – Mr. Wynn said he also was unable to account for the accident, excepting that the hook had not been properly put into the link of the chain, as stated by last witness.

Some conversation then ensued between the coroner, the inspector and Mr. Anstice, as to the suggestion of putting the hook under the bonnet, a plan which was ultimately thought to be impracticable. One of the jurymen remarked that he had come up with another on the point of the hook himself. Mr. Anstice said the hooker-on who, poor fellow, was among the killed, was an experienced hooker-on, and had filled that office for twenty years. James Davies said he was manager at the Lane or Brick Kiln Leasow Pit, and that the hooker-on at the pit, Benjamin Davies, was the responsible person; Wallet and Tranter also had the underground management of the workings, and they were also among the killed. This was the whole of the evidence, and the jury without hesitation, returned a verdict of 'Accidental death'.

The funeral of the miners was one of those occasions where ceremony was of vital importance to the many who had been bereaved or affected by the enormity of the disaster. One of the newspapers reported it thus:

THE FUNERAL OF THE DECEASED MEN

The remains of the poor fellows that perished in so shocking a manner were interred in Madeley churchyard on Saturday last. The church and its vicinity was crowded with persons anxious to see the end of the deceased, each followed by mourners, two abreast where a single corpse was conveyed, and four ditto where there were two. The whole of the pits in the field ceased working at midday, in order that the men might attend, and upwards of 400 did so, making altogether, including the relatives and friends of the deceased, about 500. We also observed … about 2000 persons assembled in the churchyard. The church was crowded, and as the coffins were being placed along the aisle the organist played the "Dead March" in Saul. The burial service was impressively read by the Vicar, the Rev. G.E. Yate. The funeral party then proceeded to the grave, preceded by the vicar, reading the burial service in a solemn and impressive manner. The grave was one of unusual dimensions, being nearly 16 feet by six feet, in order to receive the whole of the coffins. Some difficulty was experienced in finding room for the relatives of the deceased owing to the crowd, but the greatest decorum was observed; and the bodies were conveyed to their final resting place amid the audible sobs and sighs of the mourners. The ceremony having been concluded the vast crowd dispersed to their homes, no doubt deeply impressed with the awful solemnity of the scene they had witnessed. We are informed that the Madeley-wood Company, in whose field the accident happened, have done what they could to mitigate the sorrows of the relatives, by visiting them, condoling with them, and sending substantial relief. They also took upon themselves the expenses of the funeral, providing coffins, hearses, &c. After taking note of the order in which the bodies of the unfortunates had been laid to rest, their grave was filled in and the soil allowed to settle for a short while before the area was enclosed in a fitting memorial. A local stonemason prepared a headstone in memory of the victims whose names were followed by the inscriptions:

Who were killed by the unhooking of the chains in which they were ascending the shaft of the Brick Kiln Leasow Crewstone Pit in this parish, at the end of the day's labour, on Tuesday, 27th September 1864.'

'I went to the bottom of the mountains
The earth with its bars was about me forever.
Yet hast thou brought up my life from corruption, O Lord my God. '

'When my soul fainted within me, I remembered the Lord, and my prayer came unto thee, into thine holy temple.'

'Watch, therefore, for ye know not what hour your Lord doth come.

The headstone was incorporated into one side of a low brick wall laid around the perimeter of the sacred plot. Nine long cast iron slabs, each bearing the initials of one of the victims, were cast in a local furnace and placed inside the wall above the body to which each pair of initials related. The slabs are unusual in that they are not flat, but have a triangular profile to prevent rainwater from collecting and oxidising the metal.

Finally, a cast iron fence was erected above the brickwork in order to protect the grave as well as to emphasise the importance of the event which had claimed so many lives.

15

THE SPRINGWELL PIT DISASTER, DAWLEY

The disaster at the Springwell Pit occurred on 6 December 1872. The shaft was about 150 yards deep; eight miners had attached themselves to the bottom of the triple-link chain at the end of the day and were being hauled up to the surface.

The incident took place within a few weeks of another tragedy which had taken place at Pelsall, a few miles away, an event referred to in the press reports at the time.

They had only ascended some twenty yards or so up the shaft when the triple-link chain broke, but it was enough to kill seven of the men instantly. The eighth man was brought to the pit bank but expired within a few minutes. This is the graphic report which appeared in the local press:

DECEMBER 1872

THE APPALLING PIT ACCIDENT AT DAWLEY
EIGHT LIVES LOST

It is a saying unpleasantly true that misfortunes never come singly, and the accident at the Springwell Pit on Friday last rendered the saying painfully apparent to the men of Dawley, following so quickly as it did upon the Pelsall catastrophe, in which the lives of five Dawley men were sacrificed. For years the colliers of Shropshire have been able to congratulate themselves upon a blessed immunity from pit accidents with more than single cases of fatality; but by the calamity at Little Dawley on Friday afternoon, they were ruthlessly awakened to the fact that their favoured district was not to remain exempt from casualties of a far more serious nature than has characterised those past years.

On the day in question, the men employed by the Coalbrookdale Company, and whose duty it was to extract the ironstone from the Springwell Pit, proceeded to their work, which they carried on throughout the day, without aught occurring to warn them that an event was at hand which would cut off in the very spring of life, eight of their number.

The busy engine clanked throughout the day, and the chain was sent up and down the shaft to the extent of its 150 yards length, ever and anon returning to the surface with its weighty loads of stone; and so all went on well until half-past four o'clock in the afternoon, when, instead of a heavy load of inanimate stone, a lighter, but ten thousand times more precious, load was hooked on to the chain – a "handful" of eight living men, the tired workers of the mine.

The signal was given to hoist, the chain was slowly conveying the men on the first step towards the homes they were destined never to enter again, and fifty yards of the treacherous iron rope had been wound around the drum at the engine-house when, without the slightest warning, the triple links snapped a short distance from the pit-mouth, and its living freight followed by some hundred yards of cruel, crushing chain was hurled to the bottom, where, after a few moments of mortal agony, all that left of the first "handful" of men to leave the Springwell Pit, on Friday, the 6th day of December, 1872, was a heap of seven mutilated corpses, and a maimed and rapidly expiring miner.

After the first shock had passed over those on the spot, every effort was made to ascertain the extent of the disaster, and fresh chain having been supplied, the work of bringing the bodies out of the pit was proceeded with. Directly the accident became known an anxious crowd collected on the pit bank. The dreadful nature of the disaster, however, precluded all hope that any of the men could be brought out alive; and, as after events proved, seven of the poor fellows must have met with almost instantaneous death, the only man brought out of the pit alive being the man Davies, who was at once attended to by Dr. Soame and his assistant, who did all that medical skill could devise to preserve the rapidly sinking miner, who succumbed a few moments after being brought to bank.

The bodies of the other men were shortly brought to the top, and, being placed in sacks, were taken through the narrow living lane of afflicted friends and spectators, who crowded the pit-mound to the Crown Inn, where the club-room had been prepared for their reception. As may be expected, there was a great deal of excitement caused by the sad incident, but there was not observable, to any great extent, the terrible scenes of grief and desolation that at times mark the occurrence of colliery accidents, such as those which for a time surrounded the name of Pelsall with a painful interest.

The bodies, which presented a very sickening spectacle at first sight, were ranged along the floor of the club-room, and the necessary labour of laying out and identifying the dead was proceeded with, by women selected for the purpose, who worked under assistance rendered by the Rev. Mr. Drury, curate of Dawley, who was unremitting in speaking kind words of comfort to the friends of the deceased, and otherwise rendering aid.

The melancholy task in the club-room was undertaken by Mr. Benjamin Lloyd, the landlord of the Crown Inn; Mr. Bright, grocer; and Sergeant Simcox. As the work of stripping and washing the dead proceeded far into the night the people who had remained in and about the Crown, quietly dispersed to their homes.

The first to be laid out on the temporary bier erected was the young fellow Smith, whose features seemed wrapped in the quiet repose of sleep. Next came Wyke, who had a terrible deathdealing cut on the head. Of course the whole of the men were more or less mutilated; but the injuries seemed to be principally confined to internal parts. The man Bailey, the only one married of the deceased, was sadly cut about the head, and had in addition sustained fractured arms and legs. The poor lad Skelton, whom we have been informed was brought out of the pit in his father's arms, presented a shocking sight.

The following is a complete return of the dead:

John Davies (19), filler, Brandlee.
Edward Jones (21), miner, Stocking.
Isaiah Skelton (15), miner, Little Dawley.
Allen Wyke (20), miner, Finney.
Robert Smith (18), miner, Holley Hedge.
William Bailey (21, married), miner, Finney.
John Parker (22), miner, Holly Hedge.
John Yale (21), miner, Dawley.

It will be seen that, with one exception, the whole of the above were single men, but while only one widow and an orphan are left to mourn a husband and a father, the accident will prove an irreparable loss to several families; and it is to be hoped that the generous promptitude which caused subscriptions to flow from Dawley towards Pelsall will again influence the conduct of the inhabitants under the present circumstances. It is singularly co-incidental that five of the number killed at Pelsall were natives of Dawley, and at the time of this accident the Rev. R.C. Wanstall, the vicar, was absent at Pelsall, taking the money raised in his own parish for the relief of those in Staffordshire. The rev. gentleman has lost no time in appealing to the public for subscriptions towards the sufferers at Little Dawley, and we feel in duty bound to re-produce the letter which has already appeared in several newspapers:

TO THE EDITOR

SIR – In your paper of to-day you briefly allude to the appalling pit accident in this parish, whereby eight young men lost their lives by the snapping of the winding chain while drawing them up. Now that the public mind is so roused in reference to the sad catastrophe at the Pelsall Colliery, I do trust some aid will be manifested to these in this parish who are likely to suffer very considerably by the fatal accident referred to. Although only one of the men in question leaves a widow and family, yet three or four of those who have come to so untimely an end were, in a great measure, the support of their several families. Collections are being made in this district for those bereaved by the Pelsall Colliery disaster, and I rejoice to say that our people are giving "according to their ability." Under these circumstances I would earnestly solicit help from the general fund now being raised, so that the really deserving in the recent "Dawley pit accident" may partake of the liberality now being manifested to our bereaved brethren at Pelsall. – Believe me, your obedient servant,
E COTTERILL WANSTALL
Vicar of Dawley. Salop. The Vicarage, Dawley, Dec. 7.

THE INQUEST

On Saturday, Mr. J. Wynne, one of her Majesty's Inspectors of Mines, visited the Springwell Pit and examined the broken chain. He complained, however, that only one of the three broken links immediately causing the accident could be found. This link presents the appearance of being much worn; but of course as a searching inquiry will be made into the matter, it was not deemed advisable to take any evidence on this point. Mr. Wynne caused about 13 yards of the chain to be cut from the whole length, several of which were tested, the opinion of the inspector upon the examination being reserved until the adjourned inquest.

R.D. Newill, Esq., coroner, opened his inquiry at the Crown Inn, Little Dawley, when the following gentlemen were sworn on the jury: – Messrs Noah Wilkes (foreman), R.D. Sammers, T. Garbett, H. Jones, J. Bright, T. Bray, F. Ketley, W.H. Jones, R. Mainwaring, James Rushton, O. Huffedine, Thomas Keay, R. Rowley, W. Davies, and John Fisher.

After being sworn, the jurymen preceded to view the bodies, which, all laid out, as they were, in snow-white funereal raiment, presented a sight not easily to be forgotten by the most callous. A painful scene was witnessed here by the presence of the fathers of four of the unfortunate victims, who, with grief-stricken pertinacity, refused to leave their dead; an occasional stifled sob or moan telling only too plainly the acuteness of their feelings under their new affliction. The clergymen of the parish were present, administering spiritual comfort to the bereaved, but in some instances their efforts were unavailing. Upon return to the room where the inquest was being held, Mr. Newill intimated that he should only take evidence relating to the identification of the bodies on the present occasion. William Wylde was then called. He said he was a chartermaster engaged at the Springwell Pit. He knew the whole of the deceased, and they worked at the pit in question. He had seen the bodies, and identified them (as given above). He saw the men brought up out of the pit; they were all dead with the exception of Davies. The Coroner said that was all the evidence he intended taking then, and the inquest would be adjourned; in the meantime every inquiry would be made, and he had no doubt that at their next inquest they would be able to complete the case.

Martin Cooper, miners' agent, asked whether it was true that eighteen men had refused to go down the pit because the chain was not considered safe? and whether summonses had not been taken out against them for so refusing? The Coroner said that was a matter that could not be entered upon then.

Mr. Wynne informed Cooper that if he had any evidence to bring forward in support of what he stated, to be prepared with it at the adjourned inquest. The inquest was then adjourned until Tuesday next.

The pit at which the accident occurred is situated about 600 or 700 yards from the parish church of Dawley, in the village of Little Dawley, and is one of a group worked by the Coalbrookdale Company, a company that have ever evinced the greatest interest is the welfare of their men. At this pit, which is a "slow-winding" one, like the others in the district, the men are not drawn up in cages or tubs, but are brought to the top in what is known as "handfuls" that is, the men attach themselves by chains, in which they sit, to a link fixed at the end of the shaft chain.

The system, we believe, is only adopted in Shropshire, and the term "handful" is a purely local term. From particulars gleaned upon the spot, it appeared that the demeanour and general conduct of the men in life was considered to be, by those who knew them, most exemplary; some of them being regular attendants at the Dawley night school, where their efforts to learn met with the warm approval of their master, Mr. Woodhouse. The young fellow Parker was an attendant of the Sunday School; and here again it is pleasing to record that he evidently stored up what he heard there, for, but a fortnight before his untimely death, he had heard the Rev. Mr. Drury read from a book called "He is overhead," the contents of which he was so much delighted with that he secured a copy, and at meal-times, in the pit, he used to read extracts from it to his fellow workmen.

The continuation of the inquest concentrated on the state of the chains in use at the pit and whose responsibility it was to check their condition and make repairs. Furthermore, why had not a new spare chain been put to use when the uncertain condition of the damaged chain became known?

The poor condition of the chain had been mentioned by the workers a few days before the accident. They were, understandably, afraid to descend into the pit. Some work had been done to repair the lining of the shaft (a few bricks had worked loose and there was a possibility that they could have fallen on top of anyone below) which meant that the shaft was closed for a day. During that time the banksman had noticed a weak link in the chain and had marked it for repair. One of the two chartermasters at the pit, William Wylde, was adamant that he had instructed the banksman Morris to examine the chain thoroughly and several rivets were inserted by way of repair. Despite this action, some of the men were still very nervous. Wylde was equally adamant that he had received no complaints from the men. The jury disagreed.

Work resumed in the pit the following day and the accident occurred. Various people gave evidence, including the Inspector of Mines. Accusations and denials were made by everyone involved. It was even asserted by the pit manager that the cause of the accident lay with the young men who had been swinging to and fro on the chains to frighten the others; the chain could have twisted and snap. This assertion was dismissed, even though such 'playful' activities were commonplace.

Eventually the jury delivered its verdict: 'the deceased were killed by the breaking of a chain.' William Heighway (the Coalbrookdale Company's engineer) and Henry Rawson (the Company's overall pit manager) were severely criticised by both the jury and the coroner: 'You systematically neglected your duties' and 'a joint responsibility rests with you.' No criminal charges were brought.

The funeral of the deceased was one of those rare dramatic occasions attended by an incredible number of people. Considering the amount of information written, it reflects well upon the importance of accuracy when reporting major events for the newspaper.

THE FUNERAL

Of the poor fellows killed on Friday took place on Tuesday afternoon last (10th December), at half past two o'clock, in the graveyard at Dawley Church. Long before the time appointed for the last sad ceremony to be performed, thousands had flocked into the little village of Dawley Parva, a dense crowd filling the open space in front of the Crown, where the bodies found their last temporary resting-place. The scene throughout the village of Dawley and the adjacent neighbourhoods was one of general mourning, and must be accepted as proof of the heartfelt sympathy of the whole of the district, mining population in particular, and inhabitants generally, with the families of those about to be consigned to their last resting-place.

The whole of the shops in Dawley were closed, and those houses having no shutters put up exhibited the usual sign of mourning by lowering their blinds; not a cottage but observed this mark of condolence. The day was one of those dull, foggy days natural to the month of December, and whatever was wanting to complete the universal picture of gloom was supplied by the dense mist, which hung like a funeral pall over church and graveyard, pit and road, house and shop, street and alley, the only objects imbued with life being the wayfarers, who, in silent hundreds, wended their way to the spot where the last act of the Springwell tragedy was about to be enacted.

From every point, the crowds kept flocking into the churchyard, where they took up

Holy Trinity church, Dawley, rebuilt 1845, and the communal grave of the eight miners killed in the Springwell Pit Disaster. Note the massive pit mound behind the church.

advantageous positions for viewing the funeral cortege as it arrived, or, after brief glimpses at the vault so soon to contain eight of their fellows, left to swell the moving mass which filled the road between the church and the Crown, from whence the procession started.

As a moderate computation, there could not have been less than 10,000 persons present, who, despite the continued jostling against each other, and the usual inconveniences of an overwhelming crush, maintained the greatest order and decorum. Of course the visit of such numbers to view the vault – facilities for which were freely extended by the church officials – caused many a grave mound, under which some beloved one slumbered, to be much trampled upon, the traces of which must remain for many a day.

Shortly before the time appointed for the funeral procession to start for the graveyard, a hymn, in which all present joined, was sung, and as the last note died away, the Malinslee Band, playing the "Dead March," in Saul, headed the way to the church. The whole line of route was densely packed with a multitude of spectators, the majority of whom, as the cortege passed, were fain to mark their interest in the proceedings by letting unchecked tears fall, and many a horny hand that day brushed tears away form eyes unused to weep; while the women who witnessed the passing of the line of coffins were affected second only to those who mourned behind each body. As the procession hove in sight of the graveyard, the scene was one that will never be forgotten by the most callous.

Tier upon tier of living faces met the eye, and in one unbroken link the churchyard wall was packed with hundreds of sightseers, all anxious to obtain a look at the bodies as they passed. By prior arrangement, it had been decided to let none enter the church until the bodies had been deposited in the aisle, and the mourners and those taking part in the procession had been seated; and it is with a word of praise to the policemen present that we can say this arrangement was successfully carried out.

The first coffin to be brought into the church was that of the man Bailey, which was followed by those of John Parker, Edward Jones, John Yale, Alien Wyke, John Davies, Robert Smith, and the poor lad Isaiah Skelton. Placed upon coffins were immortelles (everlasting flowers). The mourners nearly filled the body of the church, the space remaining unoccupied being quickly filled to overflowing by a large and attentive assemblage, who listened with wrapt attention to the solemn sentences of the burial service, the only sounds heard in the sacred edifice after the last cadence of the "Dead March" had pealed solemnly away being the voices of the officiating ministers, the Revs. R.C. Wanstall and E.C. Drury, and the stifled sobs of the griefstricken mourners, which would at times rise to a wail from some Rachel who refused to be comforted as certain passages were read.

But more especially did poignant grief break forth during the delivery of the few remarks by the Vicar: Such a day and such an hour as this, such a sight as they had seen that day, and with such an array of corpses before him of those, who, until a day or two ago, were alive and in their midst, he felt was an occasion upon which he was called upon to say something. The whole of the bodies were then taken from the church, and deposited, beneath the deepening twilight, in the vault prepared for this purpose. The scene was here, again, most affecting, and after a last lingering look, mourners, friends, and spectators dispersed to their homes, better, it is to be hoped, than they left them.

The arrangements for the funeral were most satisfactorily carried out under the direction of the Coalbrookdale Company. Among those present at the funeral were W.G. Norris, Esq., and Mr. Rawson, colliery manager. Subscriptions are earnestly solicited in aid of the bereaved families by the Rev. R.C. Wanstall.

16

THE DONNINGTON WOOD PIT DISASTER

1875 was not a good year for colliers in the Donnington Wood area. As usual, there had been several accidents, one of which resulted in the deaths of three men at a pit near the impressive Lodge Furnaces in June of that year (see Chapter 12). Broken chains were the cause.

This latest disaster, which took place on 11 September 1875, should have been avoided. Eleven miners and a horse died because of gas poisoning. The men had been lowered to the bottom of the shaft where they waited at the entrance to the mine (the 'inset'). It was sometimes the practice, as on this occasion, to then await the lowering of one of the pit ponies, and the men below would unfasten the horse from its chain harness, ready for work. Finally, the pit 'fireman' would descend with his safety lamp and carry out an inspection of the mine, checking for the presence of toxic gases, before the men were permitted to go about their business.

This time it all went horribly wrong. In theory, the fireman should have been first to be lowered into the pit to check all was safe before anyone else descended. On this occasion, it was asserted that the first two batches of men had given the usual signal when they reached the bottom of the shaft. By the time the horse was lowered, all the men were dead, overcome by fumes. The horse died while still in its chain harness, dangling in mid-air. The fireman arrived too late to change the outcome of events. Apparently, this had previously been regarded as a 'safe' pit.

The bravery of those who risked their own lives in order to recover the bodies cannot be praised too highly. Colliers lived in constant danger while digging away in the most primitive conditions, but it requires a different kind of courage to descend into the dark when the cause of the deaths is not yet known. Their knowledge of the mine layout, together with the ingenious method adopted for the recovery, can only be admired. The only criticism of the actual scene of the incident was that tactfully voiced by the coroner at the inquest; after the bodies had been recovered they 'were moved to their separate homes by their sorrowing relatives', whereas they should all have been carried to a single location, such as a nearby public house or a suitable alternative suggested by the pit owners. This measure was essentially there to assist the coroner with the identification of the bodies.

SEPTEMBER 1875
TERRIBLE COLLIERY ACCIDENT AT DONINGTON WOOD
ELEVEN LIVES LOST

One of the most appalling calamities which it has ever been our painful duty to record in connection with the Shropshire coalfield occurred on Saturday morning last, by which eleven unfortunate miners were, without a moment's warning, hurried into eternity. The scene of the dire catastrophe was the pit chartered by Mr. Henry Guy, in the Donnington

Wood Colliery, belonging to the Lilleshall Company.

At six o'clock, the pit's company assembled on the bank for the purpose of descending to their work, and a detachment of six men went down first. No signal was given by them, and five others were directly afterwards lowered, those on the bank not suspecting, of course, that anything was the matter, the sinkers having been down on the previous night and reported all safe. Henry Guy, the chartermaster, remained on the top, with three men for whom he could not find work. After the eleven miners had descended, a horse was let down.

No one, however, was at the bottom of the shaft to receive it, nor did the shouts of Guy and his helpers at the top meet with any response. It then became evident that something alarming had happened, and a descent was made by the down-cast shaft. This revealed the fact that a portion of the pit had fired, and that it was full of poisonous gases.

The alarm spread with great rapidity, and the pit bank was quickly thronged, not only with men willing to risk their own lives in seeking for what must prove the corpses of relatives, friends and neighbours, but likewise by women, frantic with grief because of the sudden desolation which had fallen upon them. By 'bratticing,' and by re-opening a road twelve yards in length, which had become filled up with debris, it became possible to pass from the bottom of one shaft to the bottom of the other. In effecting this, much risk was run by the workers, who now and again had to leave and return to bank, stupefied by the poisonous gas, which the little air they could alone carry with them by the aid of the bratticing was insufficient to sweep out. Presently the carcass of the horse was come upon at the bottom of the up-cast shaft, and beneath the animal there were the dead but unmutilated bodies of the two miners who had been told off to receive the animal so soon as it had been let down. The other nine miners, there was reason to believe, were all lying dead in the 'inset,' about 25 yards from the bottom of the up-cast shaft.

Upon descending, it would be their duty to remain there until the fireman, who was one of their party, had gone round the workings with his test lamp, and reported all safe. It was not possible, even with all the temporary means available, directed by men of science and of skill, to get air that could sustain life at any nearer point to the deceased than seven yards; and as the air beyond that point could be respired for only a few moments, so no light could long live in it. Through this deadly seven yards, one or other of the heroic miners who constituted the forlorn hope rushed, groping with outstretched hands, trusting that he might clutch a body and drag it into the air and light. Again and again these noble fellows succeeded, and again and again they failed to succeed. Dead miners and half dead rescuers were sent alternately to the attendants who thronged the bank at the top of the downcast shaft.

Surgical aid was there, and it proved of great service in restoring the unconscious miners who so nobly worked to reach their dead comrades. It was noon before the last body was brought to the bank. At one time intense excitement was caused by a report that one of the poor fellows was alive, but the surgeon (Mr. Gibson, assistant to Dr. Greene) soon dispersed the last ray of hope; The man was beyond all human aid. All had been fatally poisoned within perhaps ten minutes of their reaching the 'inset.'

On none of the dead was there any distortion of either features or limbs; but the lamp-black around the nostrils was a clear indication that they had breathed 'fire-stink' and carbonate oxide. Further exploration revealed that this had come from accidentally fired-coal, which was burning slowly in an air-way, some 80 yards off. The pit is working the yard coal and the yellow stone, and there is an old and closed-up working in a seam whose floor comes upon the roof of the air-way mentioned. In this old working there was an accumulation of 'gob,' or refuse slack coal, which not unfrequently ignites by spontaneous combustion. Such an ignition would seem to have occurred in this instance, and the slack, after smouldering for some days, burnt its way during Friday night through the roof of the air-way, where, as it met the air, the incandescent mass burst into a smouldering flame, which consumed the air and sent out smoke and 'fire-stink' and carbonate oxide. This vapour was deadly in the inset, as well as from thence to the seat of the fire; and by the firing of it at the naked candles which the nine who entered the inset carried, the air from the inset to the shaft, and, indeed, some distance up the shaft, became equally deadly, and occasioned the death of the two men at the bottom of the shaft and also of the horse, almost simultaneously with the death of the nine who had gone twenty-five yards further in.

Mr. Charles Green, manager of the Donington Colliery for the Lilleshall Company, was early at the pit, directing the operations for the bringing out of the bodies. The underground operations were personally directed by Mr. George Wheeler (mechanical engineer to the Lilleshall Company), assisted by Mr. A.H. Maurice (manager of the company's Priorslee Colliery), who incurred considerable risk and sustained temporary injury from the effects of the poisonous gas.

Among the other brave fellows composing the rescuing party were William Poppitt (the head sinker), Samuel Oliver, Jabez Pickering, Thomas Brothwood, Robert Shepherd, James Hancox, James Williams, Thomas Hart, Moses Pitchford, William Lowe, William Wakeley, John Leake, William Dorricott, Jabez Dorricott, John Fenn, Jonah Ball, William Pitchford, Thomas Pitchford, Arthur Cooper, and Thomas Hayward (father of one of the deceased). The Rev. G. Todd, vicar of Wrockwardine Wood, was at the pit, and asked to be allowed to descend the down-cast shaft to assist in the search for the bodies, but Mr. Wheeler had a sufficient number of men for the work. Mr. Todd, however, rendered valuable service by administering brandy to those of the rescuing party who were suffering from the effects of the poisonous atmosphere. The Rev. Mr. Hempfield and the Rev. J. Causland were also on the bank ready to render any assistance in their power. All the bodies were removed to their respective homes by their sorrowing relatives. On Sunday, Mr. T. Wynne, the Government inspector, went to the pit, which was visited by large numbers during the day.

The following is a list of

THE DEAD

James Icke, Donington Wood.

Alfred Guy, Wrockwardine Wood.

James Morgan, Wrockwardine Wood.

Charles Hayward, Wrockwardine Wood.

Daniel Guy, St. George's.

Arnold Guy, St. George's.

John White, Donington Wood.

Joseph Wagg, Donington Wood.

John Stanworth, St. George's.

Emmanuel Guy, St. George's.

James Guy, Oakengates.

THE INQUEST

The inquest on the bodies was opened on Monday, at the George Inn, St. George's, before R.D. Newill, Esq., coroner. The coroner, in opening the inquiry referred to the fact that very recently an inquest had been held upon the bodies of three men who were killed through the breaking of a chain in one of the company's pits, and expressed his deep regret that they should have been again called together so soon to investigate a still more sad and serious calamity. It would not be possible for them to conclude the inquiry that day, and if possible, it would not be right to do so, as he felt sure the jury would agree with him in saying that in a case of such magnitude it was peculiarly essential that they should obtain all the evidence it was possible to secure.

A considerable amount of feeling had naturally been caused among the friends and relatives of the deceased, and it would be better for the inquiry to stand over until a thorough investigation had been made, enabling them to find out, as far as possible, the cause of the lamentable event. Under these circumstances, he thought it desirable they should adjourn the inquiry for about a week, after the jury had viewed the bodies, and evidence of identification had been given. Before doing so, however, he had one objection to make. It was very important in cases of that kind the whole of the bodies should be removed to some central place, and it was a matter of regret that this had not been done on the present occasion. It appeared from a conversation he had had with Mr. Lloyd that a suitable place had been provided by the Lilleshall Company, and if that had been made use of it would have saved the jury a long and painful investigation, and also have saved the relatives the additional pain of the jury visiting their houses. It was not only most desirable in the interests of the public that the bodies should have been removed to some central place, but it was illegal to do otherwise, as the law required that, in the event of no more suitable place being provided, the dead should be removed to the nearest public-house. Very rarely would it happen that when such a number of persons were killed they should all lie, as in the present case, in the jurisdiction of one coroner, and it might have been that as many as four or five inquests would have had to be held. He hoped this warning would not be necessary on a future occasion.

The jury then proceeded in a waggonette to the respective homes of the deceased miners, and went through the painful duty of viewing the bodies. All lay as in placid sleep; and there had been very conspicuous indications upon their faces – some of them being quite black – of the distillation of the coal, which gave off the carbonic oxide that deprived them of life, almost within a second of its respiration. Of the deceased two were the brother and nephew, one the brother-in-law, and two others relatives of the chartermaster Guy.

It transpired that by the aid of the bratticing Mr. Wynne and Mr. Gilroy had succeeded in getting to where the men had been found; and that the mining engineers were now engaged carrying forward the bratticing to a point at which a door could be opened, and thus rapid progress be made in the afterwork of the mines, which is aimed at putting out the fire in the workings at the point where the smouldering slack in the old double-coal workings, which had been closed for 34 years, broke through.

The suspicion at present is that the air got to the smouldering slack which lay over the roof of the air-way by a crack having occurred in the roof, or by a fall of roof having taken wind to the incandescent slack, and so fanned it into flame. All this may have happened very shortly before the deceased went down. On the return of the jury, the identification of the bodies was proceeded with. The jury, after a few remarks, was left for a short time, when the following verdict was returned: "That the deceased came by their deaths, accidentally, through obnoxious gases in the Lodge Pit, but that the second bandful might have been saved if the proper signal had been given." In answer to the Coroner, the jury stated they were of opinion the signal was not given. A very kind letter was then read from Mr. Lloyd, expressing the sympathy of Earl Granville and other members of the company with the widows and orphans of the deceased, and that his lordship had enquired what could be done for their relief.

Separate funeral services for the victims followed, after which they were laid to rest in individual graves. One of the funerals included the bodies of five of the deceased and was held at St. George's Parish Church with an astonishing number of attendees.

FUNERAL OF THE DECEASED

The funeral of five of the sufferers from the recent accident took place on Tuesday at St. George's Church – John Stanworth, Emmanuel Guy, Daniel Guy, Arnold Guy, and Alfred Guy. The time fixed for the interment of the first four was three o'clock, and by that time the church and churchyard were thronged with people.

Stanworth's was the first funeral to enter the church, but was immediately followed by that of Emmanuel Guy, each being accompanied by a large number of sympathising friends. Afterwards Daniel and Arnold Guy's funeral cortege came into view. This procession was the most imposing, and was preceded by the Rev. J.R. Conor (Vicar), the Rev. J. Causland (Primitive Methodist minister), and the Rev. G. Chesson (Wesleyan Methodist minister). Then followed senior teachers of the Primitive Methodist Sunday school, then the junior members and scholars, Arnold being a Sunday-school teacher and member of that body, while Daniel was a scholar.

The Rev. R. Hempfield then commenced to read the funeral service in a most impressive manner ... In conclusion he expressed his own sympathy, and also that of the directors and manager of the Lilleshall Company, with the Mourners, and made an earnest appeal to them to seek consolation from above, and adjured the careless ones to take warning by the melancholy accident that had brought them together.

As the funeral was leaving the church, Mr. F. Tucker, who presided at the organ, played the 'Dead March' in Saul. The pulpit communion table, and reading desk, were draped in black, and the service throughout was of a most impressive character. Immediately at the close of this service, the funeral of Alfred Guy took place, the body being followed by the members of a Foresters' Court. It is estimated that between four and five thousand people were present on the melancholy occasion.

'Death is the only constant in Life.'

17
FURTHER READING

BOOKS:
Bailey, B. *Churchyards of England and Wales*
Brendon, V *The Age of Reform 1820-1850*
Burne, C.S. *Shropshire Folklore*
Dickens, C. *A Christmas Carol, Martin Chuzzlewit and Oliver Twist*
Frost, A. *The Life of Hesba Stretton, 1832-1911*
Frost, A. *The Story of Barbers, established 1848*
Frost, A. *Wellington Shreds (and Patches)*
Glover, G. *Shropshire Murders*
Harrison, J.F.C. *Late Victorian Britain 1875-1901*
Kastenburg, R and Aisenberg, R. *The Psychology of Death*
Kightly, C. *The Customs and Ceremonies of Britain*
Litten, J. *The English Way of Death*
Opie & Tatem (Ed.). *A Dictionary of Superstitions*
Richardson, R. *Death, Dissection and the Destitute*
Rose, M.E. *The Relief of Poverty 1834-1914*
Sauvain, P. *British Economic and Social History 1750-1870*
Sauvain, P. *British Economic and Social History 1850 to the present day*
The Victoria History of Shropshire, Volume XI: Telford
Wheeler, M. *Heaven, Hell and the Victorians*

DIRECTORIES, NEWSPAPERS AND MISCELLENA:
Eddowes' Salopian Journal
Harrod's, Kelly's, Mercer & Crocker's, Pigot & Co's and Robson's Directories of Salop / Shropshire, various years
Rules, Orders & Regulations of Shrewsbury Gaol, 1843
Punch magazines, various years
Shrewsbury Chronicle, various years
Shropshire Conservative, various years
Hobson's Wellington & District Directory, Almanack & Diary, various years
Wellington Journal & Shrewsbury News, various years